Karen Gottesman is the mother of eleven-year-old twins and the author of *The First Year®—Scleroderma.* She lives with her family in Pacific Palisades, California.

RAISING TWINS after the FIRST YEAR

Everything You Need to Know about Bringing Up Twins—from Toddlers to Preteens

KAREN GOTTESMAN

Marlowe & Company
New York

Raising Twins after the First Year:

Everything You Need to Know about Bringing Up Twins—from Toddlers to Preteens

Published by
Marlowe & Company
An Imprint of Avalon Publishing Group Incorporated
245 West 17th Street • 11th floor
New York, NY 10011

Library of Congress Cataloging-in-Publication Data is available.

ISBN: 1-56924-338-7
ISBN-13: 978-1-56924-338-1

9 8 7 6 5 4 3 2 1

Designed by Maria E. Torres
Printed in the United States of America

For Evan and Maya,
My twin Northstars.

CONTENTS

INTRODUCTION | *1*

AGE 1 — *11*

You Survived Your First Year, Now What?

Time to Put Your Running Shoes On

AGE 2 — *31*

The Terrible Twos Times Two . . . Fact or Fiction?

Managing Your Two Contrarians

AGE 3 — *47*

Preschool—Are *You* Ready?

Oh Yeah, What about Potty Training?

AGE 1 to 3 TRICKS OF THE TRADE — *71*

Traveling with Toddlers—A Survival Guide

Eating Out: How Not to Get Kicked Out of Your Favorite Restaurant

Cryptophasia aka Twin Language—Does It Really Exist?

AGE 4 — *87*

Out of Control, Out of Bounds

Your Twins Have Their Own Preferences Now

Learning to Tame Your Two Devils

AGE 5 105
Devils Turned Angels
Big Kid School—Together or Apart?

AGE 4 to 6 TRICKS OF THE TRADE 131
Twin Rivalry, Sibling Rivalry—The Attention Game
How's Your Marriage Holding Up?
Going Back to Work . . . Or Not

AGE 6 to 8 165
Surviving Your Twins' Multiple Moods
Keeping Up with Your Adventurous Dynamic Duo

AGE 9 to 10 193
Double Your Pleasure, Double Your Fun
Smooth Sailing, Home Free

AGE 6 to 10 REALITY CHECK 215
Dealing with Divorce, Special Needs and Other Crises
Twin Types: Identicals vs. Fraternals
This Ain't So Bad Now (Til Adolescence, That Is)

RESOURCES | 243
ACKNOWLEDGMENTS | 253
INDEX | 255

Introduction

This being an introduction, I'd like to take a moment to tell you about myself. I am the single mother of eleven-year-old boy/girl fraternal twins, Maya and Evan. They are as much alike as they are different. Maya has blond hair and blue eyes; Evan has brown hair and brown eyes. They can be laughing conspiratorially together one minute and fist fighting the next. They have exactly the same sense of humor, yet delight in different things. Both are talented, but in entirely different ways. Evan is insightful, creative, and wickedly funny. Maya is artistic, graceful, and as strong-willed as they come. They can make each other giggle with just one look or infuriate each other without saying a word. And when they get going on something together, it's as if no one else around them exists. They have been, and continue to be, the joy of my life. I've been a single mom since my twins were toddlers and seem to have weathered the storm fairly well—from my perspective, anyway. Ask my children and you might get an entirely different story. I also have an autoimmune disease called scleroderma. You've probably never heard of it. How has it affected my ability to parent? I'll put it this way: it's nothing a little chemotherapy can't help. But that was the subject of my *last* book. I won't bore you with the details in this one. I must be an anomaly in some statistics book somewhere: divorced with twins *and* a disease. If you're a statistician and can figure that one out, please let me know.

The intrigue of twins

Twins have always been a source of fascination. The Bible and mythology are full of twins. Famous mythological twins include Romelus and Remus, Castor and Pollux, and Apollo and Diana, while famous biblical twins include Jacob and Esau and Perez and Zerah. And surely most everyone has heard of Chang and Eng: the original Siamese twins (or today's preferable PC term, "conjoined" twins) born in 1811 and connected by the breastbone. The fascination with twins continues in today's world. The media seems to be obsessed with the most famous of the famous: the Bush twins, the Olsen twins, Julia Roberts's twins, even twins we didn't know were twins. Like Elvis Presley and Liberace, whose twins died at birth. My own experience with having twins has reflected the world's fascination. The questions started pretty much at conception. At the top of everyone's list was a question I found to be quite nervy. I'm sure every parent of twins reading this has been asked this question at least once, if not a hundred times: "Did you have fertility treatments or are your twins natural?" I don't know how you feel about it, but my sex life is a bit too private to share with the folk who asked about it. I mean, c'mon, *I* certainly don't go around asking people how *their* children were conceived, do you? The litany of twin questions continues to this day. Can you tell them apart? Did you have in vitro? Are they identical? Are you sure they're twins? Are they double trouble? Better you than me. And the list goes on and on and on. On some days, I just smile politely and nod. On others, I'm able to respond without a tinge of sarcasm in my voice. But on the days when my sarcasm gets the best of me, I can't help but snap back, "Yep, you're right. Better *me* than you!"

What you need to know and why

Having two babies at once comes with a steep learning curve —the least of which is a new lingo. While you've probably heard some of the twin terminology, such as *zygosity* and *singleton,* you may not have a clue as to what they mean. You're not alone. Here's what you need to know and why.

In the medical and scientific world of twin research, twin types are not referred to as "identical" or "fraternal." Identical twins are known as "monozygotic" and fraternal twins are known as "dizygotic." When someone inquires about the "zygosity" of your twins, they're simply asking about twin type. As strange as it may sound, there are many parents who can't answer that question. Twin researcher Dr. Nancy L. Segal, professor of psychology at California State University, Fullerton, noted that it is not that unusual for parents to mistakenly identify their identical twins as fraternal—but not the other way around. In part, this can be explained by the fact that identical twins are not necessarily identical in every way, due to differences in their environment or to unusual events occurring soon after fertilization. But there are many important reasons why you should know the zygosity of your twins. Besides satisfying the curiosity factor, knowing what type of twins you have can aid in your understanding of their developmental and social behaviors, as the twin types are associated with varying degrees of closeness. Identical twins are more inclined to be dependent on each other than fraternal twins and tend to have similar attitudes, feelings, and reactions. Though fraternal twins tend to be closer and more dependent on each other than normal siblings, they differ from each other just as typical siblings would. Knowing this type of information can help guide you in your decisions regarding classroom placement or activities your twins may get involved in along the way. More importantly, knowing your twins' zygosity is critical when medical issues arise. From organ transplantation to determining the heredity of an illness to emergency decisions involving blood transfusions, knowing this information could potentially save a life.

The good news is that for those of you looking for answers,

there are some very reliable methods for finding out. The bad news is that many insurance companies don't cover the costs of some of the most accurate methods available, such as blood typing or DNA analysis. Other methods for determining zygosity include molecular genetic techniques such as DNA fingerprinting, or analysis of DNA buccal cells swabbed from the inside of the cheek. Simpler methods such as physical resemblance observation or examination of the placenta and fetal membranes also exist, though they're a lot less reliable. Talk to your doctor for more information on which test may be best for your twins.

Another word you'll hear in the world of twins is *singleton*. The word is used in reference to multiples and simply means an individual member or thing distinct from others grouped with it. In our world, singleton refers to *one* baby instead of two. Another phrase you may have heard is *vanishing twin*. This refers to the phenomenon in which two embryos are detected on the first ultrasound, but only one is detected on a subsequent ultrasound. The missing embryo is thought to have been reabsorbed by the mother or spontaneously aborted, leaving little or no trace of its existence. The result is a normal singleton pregnancy. While estimates vary as to the number of pregnancies that begin with twins, scientists have confirmed that the number of twin conceptions greatly outnumbers the number of twin births.

Bet you didn't know . . .

According to the 2002 National Vital Statistics Report data from the Center for Disease Control (CDC), the rate of twin births in the United States has risen 38 percent since 1990 and a whopping 65 percent since 1980. From year to year, the twin birth rate also continues its steady climb, rising 3 percent in 2002 to 31.1 per 1,000 births. There were 125,134 twin deliveries in 2002, compared with only 68,339 in 1980. Twin birth rates seem to have increased for all age groups, but the increases were most pronounced among older mothers (10 percent for women over 40). While this skyrocketing twin birth rate is presumed to be the result of increased use of fertility drugs and assisted reproductive technologies, there's more to the story. According to a study published in the March 2004 issue of *Obstetrics & Gynecology,* an estimated one-third of this increase has been attributed to the trend of increased maternal age at birth. According to the CDC, the birth rate for women 35 to 49 has risen 31 percent since 1990—and is now at its highest level in three decades. Plus, the birth rate for women 40 to 44 has more than doubled since 1981 and has increased to its highest level since 1969. The result? One out of eighteen births to women 40 to 44, and two out of nine births to women 45 to 54, were multiple births.

Where you live can also make a difference in whether you have twins or not. According to a study by the National Center for Health Statistics (NCHS), the rates for twin deliveries in Massachusetts and Connecticut were 25 percent higher than the overall national rate. But if you live in Hawaii, your chances of having multiples decreases to about 30 percent below the national rate. The time of year and number of daylight hours also has an impact. More fraternal twins are conceived in July than any other month, while January sees the fewest twin conceptions. Scientists speculate that this is probably due to the longer duration of daylight in July, which allows for a higher secretion rate of the follicle-stimulating hormone (FSH), which causes the ovulation of two eggs. For those of you wondering about identical twins, they occur much more randomly. Identical twins can appear in any family at any time with little evidence of any type of genetic link.

Interestingly enough, the rate of triplet and higher-order multiples dropped slightly, the third decline in the last four years after experiencing an increase of more than 400 percent between 1980 and 1998. This may partly be due to recommendations issued in 1999 by the American College of Obstetricians and Gynecologists (ACOG) and the American Society for Reproductive Medicine (ASRM) intended to prevent triplet/plus pregnancies due to their high risk of adverse outcome. Refinements to assisted reproductive technologies may also be contributing to the current decline in the incidence of higher-order multiple births. A recent study found that the proportion of assisted reproductive technology procedures involving the transfer of three or more embryos (a predictor of triplet/plus outcomes) actually declined between 1997 and 2000.

More fun twin facts include:

- The scientific study of twins is known as *gemellology*.

- The word *twin* is most likely derived from an ancient German word for twine, which means "two together."
- 18 to 22 percent of twins are left-handed, compared to less than 10 percent of non-twins.
- While the fingerprints of identical twins are different, identical twins exhibit almost identical brain wave patterns.
- Once you've given birth to fraternal twins, your chances of having another set is three to four times that of the general population.
- The United States has one of the highest rates of multiple births in the world, while Japan has one of the lowest.
- In 2002, the average twin was delivered more than three weeks earlier than the average singleton (35.3 weeks compared with 38.8) and weighed approximately two pounds less.
- And in case you're wondering, my twins were natural, or "spontaneously conceived," as they say.

In search of child-rearing advice

As parents today continue to search for definitive answers on how to raise their children, one thing becomes abundantly clear: they seem remarkably worried about their ability to parent. Thanks to our quest for the perfect baby (or babies) and the desire to be the perfect parent, child-care manuals have become a staple in middle-class American homes. The reality is that child-rearing "experts" have been evolving since World War II. First there was Dr. Benjamin Spock, who first published in 1946 and whose books were second in sales only to the Bible at that time. Other famous names include Dr. T. Berry Brazelton, pediatrician and author of more than thirty books, and Dr. William Sears, author of several popular baby-care manuals. The one common thread among these experts is that it seems everyone has something different to say.

Which brings me to my book and my disclaimer: I'm a parent of twins just like you. I don't claim to be an expert on twins; I'm just an incredibly good researcher with the ability to access nationally renowned twin experts and researchers and to extrapolate fascinating data and individual experiences from parents of twins all over the country. Intertwined with this information are my own personal experiences and insight. From traveling with twins (Age One to Three Tricks of the Trade), to potty training twins (Age Three), to twin-specific school-related issues (Age Five), to twin rivalry issues (Age Four to Six Tricks of the Trade), this book has something for everyone. What you *won't* find is a recipe for the "perfect" parent or the "perfect" set of twins. It doesn't exist. This book is about trusting your own unique parenting abilities and knowing your twins will love you no matter what. Sit down and read it all at once or skip around to the chapters that may be helpful to you right now. Read it year by year or situation by situation. Take from it what you need and come back to it when you're ready for more. While there are many books available on the first year with twins, very few are available on life with twins *after* the first year. This book was written to fill that void and to address the many questions and concerns specific only to those lucky enough to be members of a very exclusive club: parents of twins.

There's no doubt that raising twins is hard work. Some days are better than others—in fact, some *years* are better than others! That said, there has not been a day in my parenting journey on which I haven't felt doubly blessed and doubly lucky to be raising twins.

Here's what I've learned so far: Do trust your instincts. Do love your twins unconditionally. Don't compare one to the other. Do be consistent. Do know when to discipline and set limits. Don't expect perfection. Do have fun. It's OK to make mistakes. Be kind to yourself and learn to be forgiving. In the words of Dr. Benjamin Spock, "Trust yourself. You know more than you think you do."

AGE 1

You Survived Your First Year; Now What?

Congratulations—you made it! You've officially survived your first year with twins. And that's no easy feat, especially if you're a first-time parent. The end of the first year brings many changes, the least of which is realizing your twins have now become bona fide toddlers. Yep, that's right. You're entering the land of toddlerhood. Now, that's not to say having twin toddlers is a piece of cake. Quite the contrary. But if you've made it this far and still have some semblance of sanity left, you can get through just about anything, toddlerhood included.

It's probably a good idea to begin to childproof your home if you haven't done so already. While you'll read more about this later in the chapter, you may as well start by getting down on your hands and knees and looking at things from a toddler's point of view. (I was too tired to get down on my hands and knees and took the easy way out: I hired a "childproofing expert"—aka handyman—to do it for me. What can I say? I was exhausted! In hindsight, if I'd known how easy it was, I would have done it myself. It wasn't the first mistake I'd make as a mother of twins and it certainly wasn't the last. We all live and learn. But there's something to be said for not having to do everything yourself. When you've got twin toddlers, it's hard to find time to accomplish *anything* on your to-do list.)

Looking down the road

Child-development experts Frances Ilg, Louise Bates Ames, and Sidney Baker believe that each age has a personality of its own. They believe the very ages themselves can be both characterized and described. In fact, in their book *Child Behavior,* they have even published a "timetable," if you will, of the customary ages of equilibrium and disequilibrium in the first ten years of life. Here's my first word of caution: do not, I repeat, *do not* get caught up in trying to make sure your twins fit perfectly into each stage. Stages are constructed from the "average" behavior for each age level. Your twins may be ahead or behind of the described behavior for that particular age, which may be exactly what's normal for them. What is unique to twins is that, because you have two of them going through these stages at the same time, it's hard (more like impossible) not to compare sometimes. Case in point: My daughter took her first steps on her first birthday. My son didn't walk until he was eighteen months old. Was I concerned? You bet. But one visit to the pediatrician confirmed what I already knew deep down. If I hadn't had a point of comparison (aka twin B), I wouldn't have been so quick to rush my son off to the pediatrician to make sure his legs weren't made of rubber or he didn't have some horrible paralyzing disease. He was perfectly fine. He was just growing and developing on his own timetable, as all kids do. I was actually surprised to learn there was such a broad range of normalcy for each stage of a child's development.

All of this is not to say you should ignore your concerns. Obviously you know your kids best. If your gut is telling you something's wrong, consult your pediatrician. While having two kids at once makes us feel like we're child-development experts, we're not. Let the expert (your doctor) be the one to determine what's normal and what's not for each of your children.

This is an exciting time

Relatively speaking, age one tends to be a reasonably smooth period in most areas of behavior. But having two going through it at once can often make for a bumpy ride. Typically, you'll notice the rate of your children's physical growth slowing down a bit and an increased sophistication in their motor capacities. During this period, children begin to see that there is a relationship between their actions and the world beyond their own bodies. This is especially true for twins. It's not unusual to have one of your twins begin to bang a toy on the floor and have the other immediately join in the fun (and it's not unusual for you to single-handedly drive up the stock price of your favorite over-the-counter aspirin, either). During this year, most twins will begin to copy each other's actions. While other babies of this age participate in "parallel play" (playing side by side without interacting with each other), twins are beginning to play with each other, often to the exclusion of everyone else—including you. But that's also the good news. Their similar development stage and skill levels enable them to keep each other occupied, which is one of the great advantages for parents of twins during this time. Twins become accustomed to the continuous presence of another human being and often learn the lesson of give-and-take earlier than singleton babies. After all, they've already had to learn the hardest lesson of all: *sharing you.*

The individuality factor begins right now

Treating your twins as separate individuals will be a lifelong process. It can be especially challenging now, since their needs are so alike. However, most parents recognize the importance of treating their twins as two separate people and try to do so right from the start. Whether it's by choosing names that sound very different or by color-coding clothes, most parents are intent on helping their twins create separate identities. One of the easiest ways to individualize them at this age is to dress them differently. That's not to say many don't succumb to the cuteness factor of dressing them alike during the very early baby stage. Even I fell victim to this fashion statement once or twice when my twins were very little. And I have a boy and a girl! I can imagine how strong the urge must be with identicals. But in the long run, it's very important to emphasize their individuality. Sometimes you need to do this out of sheer necessity. Identical same-sex twins can look, act, and sound so similar at this age that you must create a way to tell them apart. My cousins David and Becky have identical twin boys and solved this problem by always dressing one of them in blue. Not only did this help the immediate family tell the boys apart (they have two other boys as well), it helped all those outside the immediate family begin to see the twins as individuals, too. When dealing with those outside the immediate family, it's also important to point out physical and/or personality differences to help others tell them apart. This is crucial. Some put nail polish on the pinkie of one baby to tell them apart. Others rely on different shoes for each child. The trick is to be consistent. Find something you're comfortable with and stick with it.

One of the most annoying hurdles you'll continually face is the way others refer to your kids as "the twins." This protracts your ultimate goal of helping your twins establish separate identities, and continues to be one of my biggest pet peeves to this day. I'm always annoyed when people say "How are the twins?" instead of "How are Maya and Evan?" If you can, try to find at least a few different ways in which you can emphasize their individuality. One tip I was given when my twins were very young was to always make sure I took separate photos of each child *in addition* to all the photos taken together. I can assure you this helps. My kids still appreciate looking at baby pictures of *just* themselves—without their twin.

Most parents of twins have at least one irrational hot button when it comes to making sure their twins are treated as two instead of one. Mine was separate birthday cakes. I was a maniac about making sure each twin had their very own birthday cake on every birthday. I mean, would you want to share your birthday cake every year? I wouldn't. Who wants to be denied the pleasure of blowing out their own candles on their birthday? Others feel strongly about having two sets of the same toys. Or not sharing clothes. Whatever your hot button is, go with it and know that in the long run, you're helping your twins to see themselves as individuals instead of a set.

Equal time may mean double frustration

Talk to any parent of twins and you'll discover one of the biggest frustrations of parenting twins: *equitable division of your time.* While this is true in all families with more than one child, it is especially true with twins. And while simply dividing your time evenly sounds like a good solution, it doesn't work. Being spontaneous about your children's needs and making sure each child has some individual time with you is pretty much the best you can do. Remember, though, that twins are very good at diverting attention away from the other. When you try to play with one child, the other may get jealous and try to interfere. Many parents feel exhausted and defeated by the competition for their attention. This is completely normal. When you've reached the end of your rope, take a five-minute time-out for yourself and try to regroup. Eventually you will be able to find the right balance between doing things together with both kids and having individual time for each child. There is light at the end of the tunnel. I promise.

Try to enjoy this time

Having twins comes with a very steep learning curve and it's often easy to forget to have some fun in the process. When I try to think of the early days with my twins, most of it's a blur. You're so busy just trying to get from one day to the next that it's easy to forget to stop and smell the roses along the way. Most parents of twins will agree: the first year is the hardest. But now that the first year is over, you'll find yourself having fewer and fewer Calgon moments. With each coming year, you'll have new challenges and frustrations, but you'll also experience new joys and magical moments. And remember: don't be afraid to ask for help if you need it. You may not have had time earlier to join a twins club or a support group and now may be a better time for you. Speaking from experience, such organizations can be a wonderful resource not only for practical information but also for moral support. Oftentimes there's nothing more comforting than being with a group of people who have been through similar experiences. Being the parent of twins is a special privilege. It's true what they say: twins are twice the work but twice the fun.

Time to Put Your Running Shoes On

Besides being ultra-organized, raising twins requires you to use a lot of common sense. But if you're anything like I was, you're probably far too exhausted to remember you even *have* common sense, let alone to use some. If you're in the same boat and can't seem to think straight, go easy on yourself; it happens to the best of us and is usually only temporary. In the meantime, allow me to be your common sense for you so you can get back to more critical issues, such as sleeping.

Childproofing your house

As I mentioned earlier in the chapter, it's important to begin to childproof your home *before* your twins begin to walk. That's when the real havoc in your house will begin. There are two ways to go about doing this. The most practical way involves assessing all the possible hazards in your home that need safeguarding, including electrical outlets, medicine cabinets, kitchen cabinets—especially those that contain cleaning products—drawers, toilets, stairs, doorknobs, and windows. Most hardware stores and baby stores carry just about every possible gadget you'll need to get the job done. Then, it's simply a matter of installing the gadgets (drawer stoppers, electrical-plug fillers, cabinet hinges, toilet-seat locks, etc.). Sounds easy enough, right? But what if you or your partner are "gadget challenged" like I am? Then, by all means, you should follow in my footsteps and hire a "childproofer" to do the work for you. As I mentioned earlier, though, if I had it to do over again, I would have figured out a way to install the stuff myself, as it really isn't all that difficult. (Then I would have taken the money I saved and gotten myself a nice massage or two.) But I actually did learn a few tricks of the trade so it wasn't a total loss. I learned that there's a gadget to stick in your VCR to prevent little fingers getting stuck in there, or anything else for that matter. I'm sure I'm not the first person ever to find goldfish or dried Play-Doh in my VCR. (I know, I know, I'm dating myself by talking about VCRs. I'm sure there's a DVD gadget out there, too.) And you know those sharp table corners that are eye level with your toddlers? Who knew what a big business rubber corner covers would turn out to be? Here's one I never thought of: the strings hanging down from window blinds. Bet you didn't know there's a little gadget out there for making these strings less hazardous. Other appealing hazards for toddlers include long phone cords, electrical cords, glass vases (or glass anything), small objects, and just about anything liquid. This includes pools. If you have a swimming pool at your house, make sure it's either covered or fenced in. And while this goes without saying, I'll say it anyway: *never* allow your toddlers to play around the pool unsupervised. You'd be surprised at how much can happen in the short amount of time it takes to answer a ringing phone or run in the house to get a snack. Nothing is as important as adult supervision around any body of water. Nothing.

Here's another thing I bet you didn't think of. Many pieces of furniture in your house, particularly shelving units and smaller pieces such as end tables or little dressers, can be toppled over in the blink of an eye. Lots of parents, especially those with twins, choose to bolt dangerous furniture to the wall or to the floor. As you well know, two together can create exponentially more mischief than one. And I mean the type of mischief you've never thought of. All of a sudden toys become weapons, and anything within arm's reach gets used as ammo. Or your twelve-foot-tall Christmas tree becomes the object of a tackling game to see who can topple it over first. Bet you didn't know good china plates can make for an awesome game of Frisbee. You get the idea. This is when you need to have your wits about you and use your common sense. If it looks like it may be a potential hazard, it probably is. Nail it, tape it, secure it, or get rid of it. Better safe than sorry. The truth of the matter is, making your home a safe environment for your twins is an ongoing process that you will revisit many times as your kids grow up. It's well worth it to try and stay one step ahead of the game, as there's nothing more important than the safety of your children.

Walking already?

There's no doubt that walking is one of the most exciting milestones for parents and toddlers alike. But as thrilling as it may be to witness those first few steps, it's also a signal to parents that life as you know it is about to drastically change. Especially for parents of twins. The good news is that even after babies take their first steps, many months may pass before they can walk with ease. Walking with ease entails successfully putting together both sensory and motor skills they've already achieved. The bad news is, well, *you* may never be able to sit in one place again. You may have a little bit of a reprieve if one twin begins to walk before the other. As I mentioned earlier in this chapter, I actually had six months' time in between my two walkers. While child-development experts say walking can begin anywhere between eleven to fifteen months, it's not uncommon for some toddlers to begin walking as early as eight months or as late as fifteen months or even later. But don't worry. No matter at what age your toddlers begin to walk, I guarantee that by the time they start school, there will be no distinguishing who walked early or who walked late.

Now that your twins are walking, they will delight in the beginnings of their independence and autonomy. And while most parents of twins look forward to the day they won't have to carry their infants anymore, this newly learned skill comes with brand-new responsibilities for you. One thing to remember is that walking means something entirely different to you than it does to your toddlers. While most adults see walking as a way to get from one place to another, toddlers see it as a new activity and will go just about anywhere to explore this new sense of freedom. Keeping your twins safe should remain the number-one priority. Never leave them unattended once they begin walking, especially outdoors. It's a well-known fact that no two toddlers will ever walk in the same direction. While some parents choose to use harnesses to control their twins in this situation, that remains a personal decision. Frankly, it was never my style. But that's up to you to decide. While your children are walking in the house, it's safer to allow them to walk barefoot, weather permitting. If they do need to wear socks or shoes, just make sure they are nonskid. This is also a good time to reevaluate some of your earlier childproofing work. It's not uncommon to find additional "trouble spots" that you might not have noticed earlier. When all is said and done, prepare yourself for a period of delightful surprises and occasional disasters. And believe me, being prepared can make all the difference in how you respond to your new little marathoners.

Speech and language development

As a parent of twins, you're probably well aware of the following fact: a higher percentage of twins than singletons may be speech delayed. While any of the factors responsible for causing this delay can also affect singletons, the reality is that twins are more prone to them. The pattern with which children develop or acquire language is the same in twins and singletons, but the cause of the delay in twins may lie in the timetable of development. Besides prematurity and/or other birth complications, the most common reason for the delay may come down to twins' unique social situation. Studies indicate that many parents tend to talk less to each twin than to a singleton baby simply due to lack of time. They also tend to answer their twins' questions more briefly and rush over mispronunciations. In general, parents of twins have less time to serve as a good model for adult language. A study conducted in 1980 found that twins tended to use shorter sentences and used less speech overall than singletons. One reason this may happen is that twins become so familiar with each other's needs, wants, and body language that they may not need proper language to communicate. They may even develop their own "secret" language, called cryptophasia or idioglossia. We'll explore the myth or reality of this unique twin language in Age One to Three Tricks of the Trade.

While the singleton's main model for language is the parent(s) or an older sibling, a twin's speech model is often their twin sibling—who speaks just as immaturely. Twins are thus more likely to reinforce each other's idiosyncrasies. This is normal and will most likely disappear as your twins get older. Remember, twins are constantly competing for your attention. They tend to speak loudly and often interrupt each other. It's not uncommon for some twins to even drop the ends of certain words in order to make their points more quickly. Not surprisingly, identical twins are at greater risk of language delay because they share the most intimate language bond. Male twins are also at greater risk simply because in the general population males are statistically more likely than females to experience language delays. The good news is that most of these adaptations tend to disappear by the age of five or six. In the meantime, here are some suggestions to help you encourage language development in your twins:

- Create as much one-on-one time as possible with each twin.
- Talk frequently to your twins and make sure to model correct language in all of your verbal exchanges.
- Make sure each twin is speaking for himself/herself.
- Read daily to your twins.
- Always try to use correct pronunciation when speaking to and around your twins.
- Don't anticipate their needs; let them be verbalized.
- Discourage habits such as interrupting or shouting for attention.
- Try to create opportunities for your twins to interact separately with other children.

It's important for parents with concerns about speech and language delay to discuss them with a pediatrician. While a lag in language development may be due merely to their twinship, there's peace of mind in hearing that from your pediatrician. Your pediatrician can also rule out any physical problems, such as hearing loss, and can determine if your child should be evaluated by a speech therapist. Therapy is more effective the sooner it is begun. If you need to explore further, you can contact the American Speech-Language-Hearing Association (see Resources at the end of the book). .

Making sure your twins' speech and language skills are developing on schedule

The National Institute on Deafness and Other Communication Disorders (NIDCD), a division of the National Institutes of Health (NIH), has published a list of age-related speech and language milestones. Please use it loosely as a reference tool, and again direct any of your concerns to your pediatrician. *Loosely* is the key word here. As usual, here's my disclaimer: obviously there are many kids who are way ahead of the game and just as many behind. If your child is behind, don't jump to any conclusions; he or she may be perfectly fine. These are just guidelines and are based on the "average" child. Remember what I went through with Evan, who learned to walk six months later than Maya? That said, keep your perspective but make sure to have your questions answered by a professional.

Birth to 5 Months

- Turns head toward a sound source
- Watches your face when you speak
- Vocalizes pleasure and displeasure (laughs, giggles, cries, fusses)
- Makes noise when talked to

6 to 11 Months

- Understands "no-no"
- Babbles (says "ba-ba-ba" or "ma-ma-ma")
- Tries to communicate by actions and gestures
- Tries to repeat your sounds

12 to 17 Months

- Attends to a book or toy for about two minutes
- Follows simple directions accompanied by gestures
- Answers simple questions nonverbally
- Points to objects, pictures, and family members
- Says two or three words to label a person or object (pronunciation may not be clear)
- Tries to imitate simple words

18 to 23 Months

- Enjoys being read to
- Follows simple commands without gestures
- Points to simple body parts such as nose
- Understands simple verbs such as "eat" and "sleep"

- Correctly pronounces most vowels and n, m, p, and h, especially in the beginning of syllables and short words; also begins to use other speech sounds
- Says eight to ten words (pronunciation may still be unclear)
- Asks for common foods by name
- Makes animal sounds such as "moo"
- Starts to combine words such as "more milk"
- Begins to use pronouns such as "mine"

24 to 36 Months

- Knows about fifty words at twenty-four months
- Knows some spatial concepts such as "in" and "on"
- Knows pronouns such as "you," "me," and "her"
- Knows descriptive words such as "big" and "happy"
- Says around forty words at twenty-four months
- Speech is becoming more accurate but may still leave off ending sounds; strangers may not be able to understand much of what is said
- Answers simple questions
- Begins to use more pronouns such as "you" and "I"
- Speaks in two- to three-word phrases
- Uses question inflection to ask for something ("My bell?")
- Begins to use plurals such as "shoes" or "socks" and regular past tense verbs such as "jumped"

36 to 48 Months

- Groups objects such as food, clothes, etc.
- Identifies colors
- Uses most speech sounds but may distort some of the more difficult sounds, such as l, r, s, sh, ch, y, v, z, and th; these sounds may not be fully mastered until age seven or eight
- Uses consonants in the beginning, middle, and ends of words; some of the more difficult consonants may be distorted but attempts to say them
- Strangers are able to understand much of what is said
- Able to describe the use of objects such as fork, car, etc.
- Has fun with language; enjoys poems and recognizes absurdities such as "Is that and elephant on your head?"
- Expresses ideas and feelings rather than just talking about the world around him or her
- Uses verbs that end in "ing" such as "walking" and "talking"
- Answers simple questions, such as, "What do you do when you are hungry?"
- Repeats sentences

Besides being an adorable age physically, this year will bring some amazing emotional developments, as well. As your twins evolve from infants to toddlers you'll witness two of the biggest milestones every parent can't wait to experience: hearing their first few words and watching them take those first few steps.

While you'll begin to recognize an ongoing theme of "be prepared" throughout this book, this is definitely one of those times. Make sure to have the video camera charged at all times right now; you don't want to miss one minute of this special time in your lives.

COMIC RELIEF FROM THE TRENCHES . . .

"OH NO, MY CHILD HAS TWO HEADS!"

Dan F. and his wife, Linda, went in for a routine ultrasound before they knew they were having twins. As the doctor was performing the test, he commented aloud on what he saw. "There's one leg, and there's the other. Oh, and I see a third. Wait a minute, there's one head . . . and there's another!" With that, Dan immediately passed out and hit his head on the examining table on his way to the floor. The paramedics were called and Dan was checked into the hospital for two days of observation. When the crisis was over, Linda said to Dan, "Honey, aren't you excited about the twins?" Dan said, "Twins? Oh, thank God! I thought we were going to have a two-headed, eight-limbed creature child!" Dan was never so relieved in his whole life. And, well, humiliated. He has never lived this down.

AGE 2

The Terrible Twos Times Two . . . Fact or Fiction?

According to child-development experts, the first half of age two is quite calm and joyous. Much to your surprise, you may find that your toddlers are much easier to deal with than they were even just a few months ago. Besides being better behaved and more confident, they can also be very loving and affectionate. Many can be warmly responsive to others and generally a pleasure to be around, leaving you to wonder if the terrible twos are just a myth. Let me be the first to warn you:

the only myth about the terrible twos is the timing of it. Whether it happens six months from now, or already started six months ago, your children will inevitably go through a period of such extreme behavior that you will wonder what type of evil beings have invaded your twins' bodies.

While experts diplomatically call this a period of "disequilibrium," I like to be more blunt: It's one of pure *torture*. Temperamentally, your twins are a mess. Their emotions often seem violent and confusing, not to mention conflicted and inflexible. They want what they want exactly when they want it. They're demanding and stubborn and seem intent on making every situation as difficult as possible. Their energy combined with their lack of cooperation will make you want to pull every hair out of your head. And here's the kicker: you've got two going through this at once (as if I have to remind you!). OK, let me back off a little. The good news is that not *all* children go through this stage. And even if your twins *do* go through this stage, as with any age, there are varying degrees of "disequilibrium." So before you decide to turn to the bottle, let's examine some of the reasons *why* your children may seem to be possessed by alien creatures. If nothing else, it will help you to realize that these alien creatures will most likely disappear just as mysteriously as they appeared.

The struggle for independence

Between their second and third birthdays, your children are experiencing phenomenal growth not only physically, but mentally and emotionally. Plus, they're just beginning to struggle for some independence. This is the time to get used to hearing the word *no*, in stereo. As your twins attempt to make independent decisions and judgment calls, the word *no* will become representative of their evolving independence from you *and* from each other. Unlike singleton children, who only have to separate from parents, twins must find a way to separate from each other, too. And while there's no set criteria that all sets of twins conform to, this separation or "individuation" process will continue to go on through the rest of their lives. The process is most prominent between the ages of one and three, and then again during adolescence. It can be quite challenging, not only to you but to your twins as well. Unfortunately, you may find your twins more aggressive right now than you'd like them to be. Biting seems to be a way in which many twin toddlers act out their aggression during this time. Remember, though, it's just a stage, and your toddlers will outgrow it. You'll read more about biting in the second half of this chapter. As complicated as this period may be, rest assured that this separation process will not break the twin bond. Your toddlers' twinship is a unique, lifelong relationship, bonding them in ways no other relationship can.

Your twins are on an emotional roller coaster (which means you are, too)

Your toddlers' emotions are quite complex during this period. It's not unusual to have your children vacillate between tears and overwhelming anxiety one minute, and a profound sense of frustration the next. As your twins struggle with their desire to be independent from you, they're also struggling with their desire to remain babies and to be protected. In fact, the emotional roller-coaster ride is so profound at this age, child-development experts often compare it to puberty. As a parent, it's hard not to want to jump in and provide comfort for your children when they're in the midst of a Sybil-like experience. But remember, a normal part of your children's development is learning how to regulate these emotions. Before you act, it's very important to evaluate the cause of the tears, tantrum, or frustration. If you rush in to comfort or help your child before they have a chance to do it themselves, you may be interfering with their attempts to succeed on their own. The ability to learn to accomplish things on their own, as well as to comfort themselves, is essential to their budding self-esteem. Experts agree that the best way to help them through this stage (besides having a lot of patience) is to show respect, empathy, and responsiveness. This will help your children develop a healthy sense of self at this age.

If your twins are experiencing a double dose of anguish right now, try to let them know that these feelings are OK. Even though you're still wondering what planet they came from, this behavior is normal. But, a bit of a warning: when they start to egg each other on during this stage, it ain't pretty. I have many memories of "monkey see, monkey do" resulting in books being pulled off every bookshelf in reach, or toilet paper strewn all over the house. My twins actually went through this particular stage at age three. In fact, a lot of the parents interviewed for this book said the same thing. Additionally, most experienced a similar dynamic between their twins during this time: the tag-team effect. Here's how it works: as your twins are in the middle of wreaking havoc in your house, you somehow are able to get control of one twin, only to have the other twin try to get him/her back on their side. This happened repeatedly in my house. Since I am a single parent, my twins must have thought I was an easy target, as I was always outnumbered. I assure you I am not, and have never been, *easy.* But the ongoing dynamic was definitely a challenge to my authority. If possible, try to have another adult around to help tame the "team." Try to separate them and get them involved in a calming activity. Read a book together. Go for a walk. Eat a healthy snack (no sugar right now). Or simply hug them or hold them until these feelings have subsided. Not only will your child benefit from the warmth and security of being in your arms, you too will benefit from the closeness of the moment.

Temper tantrums and aggression

While temper tantrums are often the result of exhaustion, frustration, or a desire for attention, keep in mind that a tantrum is not something your toddlers can prevent. Tantrums allow kids to release pent-up anger and frustration. During a tantrum, your children are overwhelmed by internal rage. This terrifies them. The two most important things to remember during a tantrum are to keep your child safe and to try to hold back your own emotions. While this is easier said than done, the following tips may help you to keep some semblance of sanity through this very trying stage:

- **Don't turn every issue into a power struggle.** You've heard the phrase "pick your battles." Unless your children are hurting themselves or someone else, sometimes it's best just to bow out and let the tantrum run its course.

- **Do not try to argue or reason with your children.** Remember, you're not dealing with rational emotions right now. When your toddlers are out of control, they're beyond reason. You'll be walking a very fine line if you try to bargain with your toddler(s). Toddlers want everything *now*. It's a lose/lose situation no matter how you look at it.

- **Don't reward the tantrum.** If your children see that their tantrum has a positive result, they will learn to throw one whenever they want their way. Not a good pattern to start, as it may stick for the long term.

- **Try to set limits.** Your children become frightened when they lose control, and setting limits will help to provide them with a sense of comfort and security by letting them know what to expect.

- **Keep an even keel.** This may actually be the most difficult goal of all. You've got two toddlers whose emotions are swirling out of control and their escalating anxiety seems to be contagious. Try to keep your emotions in check. Your anger will only exacerbate your children's eruptions. Use a gentle tone of voice. Try to speak softly. Remember, you're the grown-up. Your toddlers need you to be the one in control, not the other way around. Keep telling yourself this is just a stage, and then, after your twins have calmed down, sneak off and pound the wall or scream into a pillow.

- **Maintain a sense of humor.** At the end of the day (or many years later), some of your best stories of raising twins will come from some of the most difficult periods. This is one of those periods. It may be helpful to jot down your feelings or keep a journal of your toddlers' craziest moments and shenanigans during this time. When you've had some time to calm down and gain perspective, there's no doubt you'll find humor in just about every trying situation you've experienced for many years to come.

As you've probably already figured out, the toddler years are some of the most difficult to handle—until adolescence, that is. The best advice of all? Drink heavily and try to remain sedated.

Oops, just kidding. Do remember, though, that it's only a stage and that "this too shall pass."

Managing Your Two Contrarians

The good news is that all this defiance your toddlers are exhibiting is a normal step toward becoming independent little people as well as establishing an identity that is not only separate from you but also from each other. The bad news? You have to figure out how to get through it! While there's no magic solution to surviving life with twin toddlers, there certainly are ways to manage your life with them more effectively. Something I found useful was to try and understand things from their perspective, especially when it came to quirky stages and challenging, age-related behavior. But sometimes it takes a lesson or two before you get the hang of it. When Evan was this age, he was adamant about wearing only long-sleeve shirts. Every day. And this went on for an entire year. While this may sound OK to those of you in colder parts of the country, we live in Southern California. We wear shorts and tank tops year-round. I let the behavior slide until the summer, when I decided to flex some muscle. It really came down to a health issue: I didn't want him overheating in the hot sun. One day as we were getting ready for the beach, I decided to put a short-sleeve shirt on him. Well, you would have thought I had just put him in a straitjacket. The tirade and tears this one little change set off was beyond belief. If I had known ahead of time that this particular stage was marked by repetition (the *same* food, the *same* story, the *same* toy, the *same* clothes, etc.), I would have acted accordingly and wouldn't have been so quick to change his behavior. While this ritualistic behavior may seem rather obsessive-compulsive to an adult, it's actually quite normal behavior for a toddler. It's merely a way for your child to try to gain some control over his life. So, the lesson is that unless your child's repetitive behavior is hurting himself or others, try to put up with it as long as you can. In time, the behavior will change—just about the time, in fact, that you begin to get used to it.

Building self-esteem: don't compare twins

Rationally and intellectually, you know you should never compare twins. But this one little piece of advice, while appearing perfectly simple and easy to do, may be the hardest to follow for parents of twins. You have two children of the same age, possibly the same gender, at the same place developmentally; the setup is ripe for comparisons. Why is one taller than the other? Why is one better behaved? Why is one speaking and the other isn't? Why does one follow directions better? The list goes on and on. As hard as it may be, stop comparing. Not only is it unfair, it's unwise. And it completely undermines your toddlers' self-esteem. Make sure each child knows they're loved unconditionally—even during the toughest moments. If you can, rid yourself of any preconceived notions and expectations. Each twin is unique. Even identical twins. You need to accept and understand each child's inborn temperament and talents. Accepting and appreciating each child for who they are allows them to be able to accept *themselves* for who they are. That enables each child to begin to develop a healthy self-esteem.

The dreaded biting stage

While there are many underlying reasons why biting occurs, the reality is you will most likely experience it with one, if not both, of your twins during various stages of development. Some of the more common reasons for biting include frustration, anger, hunger, need for attention, teething, and just plain ol' crankiness. Sometimes it happens for no reason at all: biting is merely a means of expression for the preverbal child and it can be completely unintentional or occur at random. With twins, though, sometimes you need to dig a little deeper to find out why. Biting may occur more frequently due to their proximity to each other or the amount of time spent together. Other times, it's a way for your twins to establish separation. As you read earlier in this chapter, your twins are trying to separate not only from you right now, but also from each other. Biting may be an attempt to do just that. Whether the biting involves both twins or one twin with another playmate, the best reaction you can have is to remain calm. If you overreact, it will only increase the anxiety of the situation. Make sure you let the biter know that this behavior is not OK, and also be sure to comfort the one bitten. And don't be surprised when you see tears from *both* children. Keep in mind that biting is just a stage and will certainly become less of an issue as your toddlers acquire more language skills.

Keeping the peace

As I've often said, don't get too comfortable with any one behavior pattern your children may exhibit, as it will most certainly change. While this can be quite challenging for even the most patient parent of twins, knowing this ahead of time and trying to learn why your toddlers are acting or reacting the way they are can make all the difference in your own reactions.

The following tips may help make your life a little bit more tolerable and, perhaps, even pleasant (I'm going out on a limb here . . .):

- **Enforce your authority.** Whether you feel like it or not, you *are* the boss. You set the rules and set the example.

- **Be consistent.** Knowing what's expected of them can make your children feel more confident and secure. Toddlers need boundaries, period. If you make a decision that affects your children's behavior, stick to it. There's nothing more confusing to a child than a different response to the same behavior. If you let your toddlers jump on the bed "just this once," I guarantee they are going to try it every time. Make a decision, be consistent, and don't waffle back and forth.

- **Reinforce good behavior.** A child who feels he or she doesn't get enough attention may do anything to get it. This is especially true for twins. The hitting, biting, and other aggressive behaviors may simply be a cry for attention. Make sure you're always giving plenty of attention to the *good* behavior, through praising, hugging, and talking. And try your hardest to give very little attention to the bad. In time, your twins will realize that they're able to get the reaction they want from you through the good behavior, not the bad.

- **Walk away from tantrums.** Depending on the situation, sometimes the best course of action is no action at all. Interacting with the tantrum will just prolong it. Validate their problem if you must; then just walk away. After the tantrum is over, let it go. Try not to rehash the episode or lecture your children about it. If possible, quickly move on to another activity and go about your day.

- **Give your children choices.** Don't ask your toddlers yes or no questions. If you do, you can pretty much guess the answer to the question before you even ask it. Instead, offer your toddlers choices. Just make sure they're *limited* choices.

- **Be thankful you don't have triplets.** At the end of your very worst day, remember there's always someone whose life is more difficult than yours. Count your blessings, get a good night's sleep, and be ready to start a brand-new day in the morning.

You're not alone

Let's face it. Raising twins is hard work, especially when they're at this stage. The energy it takes to get through each day is enough to exhaust even the most superhuman of us. And I'm not just talking physically. The emotional drain can also take its toll. For some parents of twins, just knowing they're not alone in their feelings is enough to make a difference. For others, it may take reaching out to parents who have gone through similar situations or feelings. Rest assured, there are many avenues to take if you feel the need for some outside support. One of the most popular is the National Organization of Mothers of Twins Clubs, Inc. (NOMOTC). NOMOTC is a nationwide support group with more than 475 clubs for parents of twins and higher-order multiples. To see if they have a support group in your area, check out their Web site at www.nomotc.org. Don't use the excuse that you don't have the time. All the people in the group are in exactly the same situation as you. It may be worth your sanity in the long run to make the time to go. And while support groups aren't for everyone, you won't know unless you try. Other resources that may be helpful include talking to a therapist (in fact, many actually specialize in raising twins), talking to other twin parents that you know personally, or talking to your own parents or a trusted friend. Sometimes it's as simple as having someone just listen to you. If the real problem is finding time for yourself, many moms of twins are very resourceful when it comes to pulling in the troops. They rely on grandparents if they're close by, babysitters, and co-op sitter pools. Believe it or not, I used to get great relief in just being able to go to the supermarket by myself. Sometimes just having that short physical break was enough to feel refreshed. Emotionally, it's not uncommon for parents of twins to experience feelings of self-doubt: *How can I give my twins as much love as one child?* But the reality is that it's no different than if you had several children of different ages. I've never spoken to a parent with more than one child who's said to me, "I don't have enough love to go around for each of my children." Believe me, your twins certainly don't feel shortchanged; this is all they know! They're going to love *you* no matter what.

The best advice I was given by a more "experienced" twin mom was to always make sure I was taking care of myself first. If you're feeling stressed, exhausted, or just plain ol' out of patience, take the time you need to rejuvenate. Even if it's just a five-minute grown-up time-out. I guarantee it will make all the difference in how you feel about yourself both as a person and as a parent. There's something to be said for the expression, "If Mom's (or Dad's) not happy, then nobody's happy." Boy, isn't that the truth.

COMIC RELIEF FROM THE TRENCHES . . .

"Our Bags Are Packed, Mom"

Kimberly S. was having one of those days. Her sixteen-month-old twins began fighting as soon as they woke up and didn't let up the entire day. Not only were they screaming at the top of their lungs, they were hitting and biting each other like cats and dogs. By early evening, Kimberly had had enough. She threw her hands up in the air and began yelling back. In the midst of her rant, she told her children, "If there's any more hitting in this house, I'm throwing everyone out." The next thing she knew, her twins were walking around the house with their backpacks on, ready to leave at any moment. The moral of the story? Be careful what you say—you never know when your twins might actually do what you ask them to!

AGE 3

Preschool—Are *You* Ready?

While the hallmark of age two is oppositional behavior (psychotic is more like it!), the hallmark of age three is socialization. You may have noticed that your toddlers have become very social animals. Your twins are now ready to look beyond their little world and reach out to a larger, more complex one.

Your twins' emerging personalities

As your twins develop a clearer sense of themselves (separate from you as well as from each other), each child begins to develop his or her own way of feeling and behaving. Even identicals. Plus, they're probably beginning to recognize themselves as twins. Compared to last year, you'll find your children to be more cooperative than they used to be, which leads to a more peaceful household environment overall. But the best news is that three-year-olds are often eager to please their parents (hallelujah!) as well as their playmates. Before you get too excited, though, remember this: all kids go through these stages at different times. As I mentioned in the last chapter, the terrible twos can occur during a fairly broad time span. They can happen earlier than age two or later than age two. My twins definitely experienced the "terrible threes." However, the next stage was easier and one of relative calm in comparison.

Your toddlers are probably beginning to feel more secure with themselves, and the word *yes* begins to re-enter their vocabulary. Plus, any ritualistic behavior (like the long-sleeve-shirt thing) your twins may have exhibited will most likely disappear or considerably lessen by this time. You'll see more smiles instead of tears, and hear *yes* more often than *no*. You'll also notice a big increase in your twins' language skills. Enjoy this period while you can, though; the typical three-and-a-half-year-old returns once again to her earlier behavior of asserting her will. On a positive note, your twins are now at an age where you have an outlet available to help foster those socialization skills (not to mention give you a little time off). It's called preschool.

What's the difference between preschool and day care?

While many of us working moms have already had the opportunity to learn the difference, here's the skinny for those of you just learning the ropes. Day care centers have schedules geared toward accommodating the needs of working parents. They typically accept babies as well as younger children. Preschools generally accept children anywhere between the ages of two and six and might have rules about your children being potty trained. While both day care centers and preschools are regulated by the same agencies and must meet the same licensing requirements, one of the biggest differences seems to be in the scheduling. A lot of preschools are exclusively half-day programs—which can be a major problem for working parents. While you may be able to find some preschools that offer extended-care options, the cost can be prohibitive, especially with twins. Remember, no one said this was going to be easy. There *are* workable solutions; sometimes you just have to be very creative to find one that works for you. When my twins were in preschool, I hired a babysitter to watch them after school. While this option can be quite pricey, it was the one that seemed to work best for my family. Finding a solution that works means peace of mind—and that's worth every penny, in my book.

Preschool is a personal decision

As with anything in life, there are no "one size fits all" solutions. What's right for one family may not be right for another, and vice versa. Preschool is no different. You may have read about "experts" who say the benefits of preschool are "indisputable." Other "experts" tout the fact that not all children need preschool if they're adequately nurtured at home. Whom do you believe? It can all be very confusing and may leave you feeling distressed over the "big decision." But the real question you should be asking yourself is, "What are the needs of my own children and my family right now?" You may surprise yourself at how quickly you come up with the answers based on circumstance alone. Say both parents need to work. Well, there's your answer right there; you have no choice but to send your twins to preschool (or some other type of child-care situation). The decision is made for you. Or, say one of your twins is physically ill. Again, your decision's already made. Now may not be the best time to start preschool, and you may want to think about it in another year or so. Or maybe *you're* the one who's not ready. You'll read more about that a little later in the chapter. For now, assuming you've made the decision that you'd like your twins to start preschool, how do you know if they're ready?

Are your twins "preschool ready"?

Now is the time to look objectively at your twins—both as individuals and as a pair. While opinion is certainly varied on the necessity of preschool, there is one thing that most experts agree on: if you decide to send your twins to preschool, send them together. Preschool involves separating from you, which is hard enough. It's probably best to allow them to begin this journey together, as they will draw comfort from being with each other. But keeping them together *now* does not mean they should stay together in the same classroom forever. Whether to separate them or keep them together is one of the most complex issues you will face as a parent. You'll read much more about this later on in the book at Age Five. The following signs are significant indicators that your children may be ready for preschool:

1. They're happy to be away from you for short periods of time.

2. They're fine being away from home.

3. They have the ability to interact comfortably with other adults.

4. They show increasing interest in other young children (besides their twin).

5. After a short observation of other children, your twins seem ready to join in.

But as a parent of twins, you have other issues to consider: What if one twin is ready and the other isn't, due to physical or social developmental delays? While there is no right or wrong answer, many parents of twins usually adopt the philosophy of "When in doubt, wait."

According to T. Berry Brazelton, an internationally known expert on child development, the following issues may be reasons to give your children additional time at home before beginning preschool:

1. Your twins exhibit slow development overall or are so-called late bloomers.

2. They were premature or had physical problems in early life including delay in physical size or development.

3. They have immature motor development.

4. They lag in social development.

5. They have difficulty with hand-eye coordination.

Any one of these factors may be reason enough to wait another year. On the other hand, while it might be helpful to read about experts' opinions, ultimately the decision is up to you. When it comes to knowing the needs of your children, no one is more of an expert than you. Trust your own judgment and do what you think is best. Remember, it's only preschool.

Choosing the right preschool

Preschool is a child's first opportunity to learn about adjusting to the outside world. And that can put a lot of pressure on a parent to choose the "right" school. Most experts agree that one of the most important things to look for in a preschool is a program geared toward social and emotional development rather than academic development. This isn't the time to worry about whether your twins are going to become doctors, lawyers, or the next copresidents of the United States. Believe me, you'll have plenty of time for that later. This is the time to focus on encouraging your children to learn how to get along in a group, follow directions, take turns, and cooperate. Basically, you want them to learn the ABCs of socialization. A good program should also be able to challenge your children intellectually and creatively *without* focusing on academics. One of the extra benefits twins receive from preschool is learning that not all children play like their twin. While your twins have always had a built-in playmate, preschool allows them the opportunity to expand their social development by interacting with other children. At this age, there's nothing so important as allowing your children to play and interact with others so they can learn about themselves as well as their peers.

Another issue you will come across when looking at preschools is the requirement that your children be toilet trained. While some children may be toilet trained by now, many aren't. Don't let this one requirement force you to toilet train your twins before they're ready. Leave that up to your children, not the preschool. Look for another. The best way to decide which preschool is best for your children is to visit each school yourself. Make a point to visit both the playground and the classroom. And always make sure to meet with the school director to have your questions answered. If all things are equal between the schools you're choosing from, your choice may come down to a gut decision: Which school feels right to you? Which teachers and administrators do you think will connect the best with your twins? And don't forget to make sure *you* get along with all those who are involved with your children. Don't underestimate your own involvement in making preschool a positive experience for your twins. A harmonious relationship right from the start will ensure an easier transition for both you and your children.

As a parent of twins, there are many additional factors you should consider:

- What is the preschool's policy regarding twins? Do they automatically separate them? And if they have a policy in place, how receptive are they to the needs of your own situation?

- Do the teachers have experience in dealing with twins? How about the administration?

- Be aware of both your toddlers' language skills. Is either child speech delayed? How will this impact their experience in preschool?

- Is one of your twins ready but not the other?

Once you've decided on the right school, it's time to be proactive about your twins' needs. Make sure you take some time to describe to the teacher the dynamic between your twins. Explain how they are alike and how they are different. Talk about any special interests and skills. If your twins are identical, it may be helpful to give them name tags or some other type of identifying feature. It can also be different shoes or different-color shirts. Not only will this make the transition easier on your children, it will help their teacher and the other kids in the class to identify your twins as separate individuals. Teachers typically don't receive special training on dealing with multiples. It's your responsibility as a parent to help the transition go as smoothly as possible.

Are you ready for preschool?

While it's easy for me to say, "Relax, it's only preschool," that's of course the luxury of hindsight. When my twins started preschool, I was a nervous wreck. And I'm a "cool as a cucumber" kind of girl. Preschool is a big deal no matter how you look at it. After all, this is a major developmental milestone for *both* you and your twins. It's normal to feel nervous, not to mention scared, freaked out, sad, and a host of other emotions. But let's get some perspective. While many parents may compare getting into preschool with getting into the right college, keep in mind there's one major difference: your kids are only *three*! In the midst of the preschool frenzy, it's easy to lose sight of the fact that you're sending your kids off for three hours of . . . *play.* Yep, that's right. All this anxiety for playtime. Now, I know I'm simplifying things a bit. But you should really try to make this experience a positive one. In the beginning, don't be surprised if your twins don't want to play with their peers. This is completely normal. And don't be surprised if they resist going. This type of reaction is usually due to the transition from home to school rather than a dislike of the school itself. But to ease your own mind, do check things out at the school to make sure there isn't anything else going on you may need to know about. As with any new situation, there is an adjustment period. Don't fret about every little detail. And don't get upset when one or both of your twins has a bad day. We all have bad days. If your kids seem to be happy overall in their new environment, then congratulations. You've just succeeded in opening up a whole new world for them, not to mention a little free time for yourself. But if you're still feeling anxious even when everything seems to be going OK, you may need to dig a little deeper to find out why. Here's a hunch: you may be feeling anxious due to the stress of the separation, especially if this is your first time being away from your twins. Chances are your twins may be feeling it, too. Read on for more tips on how to ease the transition for both you and your twins.

Easing the separation

Your readiness to separate is just as important as your twins' ability to do so. If you're not quite there yet but know it's the best thing for your children, put on a happy face even when you're feeling sad. Try not to let your kids see how anxious you are about this transition. Your twins will pick up on it, which will only heighten their own anxiety. If you can, give them the impression that you feel confident and excited about this new opportunity for them, and be supportive of their new school environment. Your support goes a long way in building your children's confidence about separating from you. Once you see your children reacting positively to their new environment, I guarantee you'll feel a whole lot better and a lot less anxious about this new step. While every preschool has their own "separation guidelines" for the first few days or weeks of school, the following tips may ease the transition:

1. If the school allows it, let your children bring something from home: a favorite blanket, a stuffed animal, even a picture of you. If the school has a policy against bringing toys from home, ask the school if your children can put it in their cubbies. Or let your children know that whatever they bring will be waiting for them in the car when school is over.

2. Plan on staying at school for the first hour or so the first few days or week. Some schools have stricter separation guidelines than others and try to lessen the amount of time it takes to separate. For some parents of twins, the separation process goes a lot quicker because the twins know they have each other after you leave. But for

others, myself included, the kids realize their twin is no substitute for Mom. Be patient. Gradually decrease the length of time you stay each day. Just when you're at the end of your rope and feel like you're a hostage at preschool, you'll realize your twins don't even know you're there anymore. But never sneak out. All that trust you just earned will go right out the window.

3. Sometimes it's useful to ask a teacher to help with the transition. If you can, arrive a little bit early so the teacher may be more available to help you.

4. Keep your good-byes short and sweet. Don't linger. And make sure to tell your kids when you'll be returning to pick them up.

5. Always pick your twins up on time. There's nothing worse than arriving at school to see your children in tears thinking you've forgotten to pick them up.

6. Get involved in the school. In fact, some co-op preschools make this a requirement. The more you know about your children's environment at school, the better you'll feel about it. And your kids will feel a tremendous amount of pride knowing their parent is helping out at school. It's a win-win situation.

At the end of the day, remember: this too is just a phase. While it all seems overwhelming and stressful right now, many years from now when your kids go off to college, you'll think back to these days with fond memories and say to yourself, "That really wasn't such a big deal after all."

Oh Yeah, What about Potty Training?

While there's much to say on the subject of toilet training twins, here's the bottom line: the single most important thing you need to know is that *only* your children can decide when they're ready to toilet train. Not you, not your partner, not your mother, and not your best friend. *Only* your child. If you abide by this mantra, you'll save yourself lots of headaches—not to mention messes to clean up. Plus, you'll be paving the road to swifter success. The second most important thing you'll need to get you through this process is patience. And lots of it. Just because *you* may be ready for your twins to be out of diapers doesn't mean they are. Each child needs to be both physically and developmentally ready for this next big step.

It would be remiss of me not to mention a current trend emerging called *infant elimination training*, which involves training babies as young as six months to signal their mothers when they are about to go. While many moms may be susceptible to the latest parenting fads, this particular one requires that you become almost obsessively attentive to your child for months on end. Realistically, is that even *possible* for a parent of multiples? I don't know about you, but when my twins were this age, I barely had the time to go to the bathroom on my own, let alone spend that kind of time helping only *one* child learn the ropes. And while I'm not a toilet-training expert, common sense leads me to believe this is a much more viable method for parents of singletons, if it is viable at all. It's probably best at this point to stick with the good old-fashioned way of toilet training until something else is proven to be better.

Signs of readiness

How do you know if a child is potty ready? Here's a list of signs to look for:

- **Capable of staying dry for several hours at a stretch.** If your children can stay dry for a few hours during the day and intermittently wake up dry from a nap, they are probably physically ready to begin the process.

- **Exhibits a sudden dislike of wet or soiled diapers.** When your children have a desire to be changed immediately out of a dirty diaper, this is a good sign.

- **Shows an interest in the toilet process, including the terminology.** When your children begin to follow you or others into the bathroom, or begin to use the toilet terminology used in your household, they're well on their way. Curiosity about bathroom activities is always a good indicator of readiness.

- **Exhibits an ability to do simple self-dressing.** Even though you're available to help, your children should be able to pull down their pants as well as pull them back up.

- **Capable of communicating their needs.** They should also be able to understand and follow simple directions.

How does this work with twins?

I remember how overwhelmed I felt at the prospect of having to toilet train not one, but two toddlers—especially as a first-time mother. If you have already been through this process with an older sibling, hats off to you. This should be a breeze. Your twins will most likely learn from copying their older sibling. Even if they don't, at least you know what to do and expect. For the rest of us rookies, well, it's another story. As with everything else that has to do with twins, there are a few additional things you'll need to know about:

1. Not all twins are ready to potty train at the same time. In general, boys tend to be ready later than girls. If you have fraternal twins of the opposite sex, don't expect them to be ready at the same time. That certainly was

the case with my twins. My daughter was toilet trained several months ahead of my son. But when he was ready, boy, did he learn quickly. On the other hand, identicals and same-sex fraternal twins often do learn at the same time because they tend to mimic each other more than opposite-sex multiples. Plus, they tend to help each other through the process. In general, twins are good role models for each other. If this isn't the case in your house, don't fret. If one twin seems interested before the other is, concentrate your efforts on the one that's ready. In time, the other twin will take the cue and want to do the same thing as the twin sibling.

2. Don't make potty training a competition between your twins. Make sure you have two potty chairs available, even if they don't train at the same time. Part of the process is getting each child used to the potty, whether they're using it or not. Keep reminding yourself that the process will be much less trying if you follow the lead of each twin. If you praise the twin that's ready, make sure you don't forget to address the other as well. Saying something simple, such as "I'm glad you're getting used to your new potty," will keep the playing field even during this time.

3. Twins can both inspire and distract each other from the task at hand. While you'll hear many stories of twins

helping each other through this stage, you'll hear just as many about twins who try to derail it. That's OK. Just try to keep them focused through positive reinforcement and rewards. You'll be amazed how quickly you can turn around a tough situation—even when you're being tag-teamed.

How can you help?

Let's start by talking about what you shouldn't do.

Don't expect too much too soon. While some children seem to master the process overnight, most don't. Try not to damage your children's self-confidence or squash their enthusiasm by setting your expectations too high.

Don't ever rush the process or force them along. Remember, this is your children's timetable, not yours. Be respectful of where they are in the process.

Don't turn this into a power struggle. There's absolutely no reason to put undue pressure on your children to get the job done.

Don't scold or punish them. While you may get frustrated when your toddlers ask to use the potty every five minutes or have an accident right after they go, try to keep your emotions in check. You can expect to take as many steps backward as you do forward. Punishment is never a solution to setbacks or accidents. Remember what I said at the beginning of the chapter? Patience, my friend, patience.

Don't nag. Most toddlers don't like to be told what to do, especially when they're learning a new skill. While an occasional reminder or a simple question asking whether they need to go is OK, make sure you don't turn into a broken record. This will almost assuredly have the opposite effect. OK, enough about what you shouldn't do. Let's talk about what you *should* do.

Do expect accidents. They're especially common when a child is stressed or exhausted. Or sometimes, they occur when a child is happily engaged in a fun activity and just "forgets" to go to the potty. It's all part of the process.

Do use positive reinforcement. Some parents like to reward their children with stickers. Some like to use praise and words of encouragement. Some parents even like to up the ante with bigger rewards as they get further into the process—but be careful how you do this. You certainly don't want to put additional pressure on your kids to "perform." Sometimes a more nonchalant attitude can help keep the activity in perspective.

Do trust your instincts. While many people in your life will be only too happy to offer useful tips that worked for their own kids, keep it in perspective. Every child is different. Even your twins are different from each other. Do what you think is right for *your* kids. You know them best.

Do have a relaxed attitude. If you find yourself becoming frustrated or putting too much pressure on your twins to succeed, back off. You'll be sending the wrong message. Most children follow their parents' cue about a situation. If your twins find you to be relaxed about potty training, most likely they'll be relaxed, too.

Do use books and videos. While there are many available on the subject, one of our favorite books was *Everyone Poops* by Taro Gomi. Another great one is called *Once Upon a Potty* by Alona Frankel. This one is especially good for those of you with boy/girl multiples as it comes in both his and hers versions.

Do realize nighttime control takes longer than daytime control. Helpful tips include restricting fluids around bedtime, making sure they use the potty right before they go to sleep, and making sure to have a plastic liner on the mattress to protect it (if you don't have one already).

Do be consistent, patient, and encouraging. The process will be a lot less trying for everyone when you just follow the lead of each child. I can't think of any better way to guarantee success.

Twin moms speak out about their potty-training experiences

Sometimes it helps to hear how other parents of twins muddled through the process. You'll find that each family has had a unique experience, just like yours.

Tami O. recalls trying to begin training her fraternal girls when they turned two years old—without success. It wasn't until a week before their third birthday that one twin decided she was ready to wear underwear. Her sister followed and both were trained from that moment on. Tami learned the hard way that it's up to your twins to decide when they're ready.

Ginny B.'s fraternal girls potty trained at the same time. Her tip? Skip the Pull-Ups (except at night). The Pull-Ups felt like diapers to her twins and actually slowed down the whole process. Once she put her girls in underwear, things went very quickly.

Meghan B. has fraternal boys and found the key to successful potty training in her house was determining what motivated each twin. While one twin needed lots of small rewards and prizes along the way, the other twin was completely self-motivated. Just getting his own potty was enough excitement and motivation for him to get the job done.

Sue L. potty trained her identical boys in two and a half months by using lots of rewards. She mostly used stickers and praise but found the best reward to be taking the boys to pick out their own "big boy" underwear. Both were delighted to be able to pick out their favorite character-decorated underwear and felt this was the best reward of all.

Isabelle R. let her identical girls run around the house au naturel. And while it took about two weeks for one twin to follow the other, both were fully trained within a couple of months.

Suzan C. tried to potty train her identical girls at the same time. She became so frustrated she had to put them both back in diapers and then waited until *they* were ready. Once they were, each potty trained—one at a time—with great success.

Jacquelyn P. bought potty seats for her identical twin boys far before they were ready to train—just to help them get used to the seats. She also put toys and books by the potty seats to make them more enticing. But she found the best tools for successful potty training to be rewards for positive behavior and encouragement following mistakes.

Julie G.'s identical girls started potty training together but one was much more interested in using the potty than the other. Ironically, the one who was more interested at first *stopped* using the potty and began to regress when her twin became successful. It became such a struggle that Julie had to use an outside resource (her pediatrician) as an incentive to help the twin who was regressing. It worked like a charm. Having the expectation of success come from someone outside the family gave her child an incentive to succeed, yet relieved her of the unpleasant task of showing parental approval or disapproval.

A few miscellaneous tips

- Put pee targets in the toilet for boys. Most baby stores carry biodegradable targets to put in your toilet, and they're well worth it. Most boys get a kick out of aiming for the targets and it gives them another incentive to use the toilet. In fact, these targets actually expedited the process for my son. He couldn't wait to use the toilet and had a ball trying to hit these targets every time he used the bathroom.

- Try using underwear instead of Pull-Ups after your twins have experienced some successes. Most parents will agree that Pull-Ups only delay the process. Most toddlers don't feel the wetness in paper Pull-Ups; they feel the wetness more easily in underwear. Plus, many toddlers are often motivated by getting "big boy" or "big girl" underwear and are thrilled at being able to choose some with their favorite character on them.

- There is no magic age to begin toilet training. While many children are ready between the ages of two and three, yours may not be. As with any developmental milestone, children must be both physically and emotionally ready to begin the task. In fact, a 2003 study from the *Journal of Pediatrics* found that children whose parents start training at a younger age actually take longer to get through the process.

- Success at toilet training is *not* a measure of successful parenting. This is not about you. This is about your children. Leave this task up to them. Your twins will ultimately master this milestone at their own speed. So put your feet up, relax, and take the pressure off. You'll be doing both you *and* your children a big favor.

In the world of twins, the prospect of "no more diapers" is a *huge* deal. Just make sure to take your cues from your children and to follow their individual timetables. The process will go much more smoothly if you follow this simple piece of advice. For those of you who are at your wits' end and think there's no end to this process, just remember: I have yet to meet a single set of coed twins who still wet their pants. Be patient and before you know it, you'll be changing your last diaper for good.

COMIC RELIEF FROM THE TRENCHES . . .

"WAIT, WHAT ABOUT *ME*?"

About six weeks after my twins were born, my husband and I thought we were finally getting this nighttime thing down. When the babies woke in the middle of the night, we had a regular routine established of having him bring each baby to me to nurse, one at a time. On this particular night, Maya woke first. After I nursed her, he put her down and within five minutes Evan woke up, waiting for his turn. Maya was still a bit restless and was now crying as loudly as Evan. In the darkness, my husband got up again to bring Evan to me for his turn to nurse. That is, he *thought* it was Evan. Between the noise, the exhaustion, and the darkness, he mistakenly brought me Maya, who was only too happy to be fed and cuddled . . . *again.* I, of course, was too exhausted to be paying attention and just assumed he had brought Evan. Maya, happy and full, immediately went right back to sleep. Evan, who had yet to be fed, was still screaming like a wild banshee. For the next hour, we were perplexed as to what the problem was, until it finally hit us! The poor little guy was starving! Well, we made sure that that *never* happened again by separating their bassinets to opposite sides of the room the very next day. We *still* laugh about it.

AGE 1 to 3
TRICKS OF THE TRADE

Traveling with Toddlers—A Survival Guide

Whether you're in a plane or a car, traveling with twin toddlers can rattle even the most patient of parents. While there's no magic solution to keeping the calm, there are definitely a few tricks of the trade to help the trip go as smoothly as possible. Let's start with airplane travel first. Unfortunately, air travel these days is not what it used to be. If you haven't flown since 9/11, you're in for a few surprises. The reality of post-9/11 travel is, the hassle factor alone is enough to convince a lot of people (especially those with children) to just stay home. Or, at the very least, find someplace to go to by car. The amount of time spent going through ticket lines, screeners, and security checkpoints is enough to make anyone think twice about their travel plans. All this *before* you even get on the airplane. It makes traveling by train sound very appealing. But before you turn to the "tracks" and give up flying altogether, read on for tips on how you and your twins can survive your next airplane flight without losing your minds.

According to the American Academy of Pediatrics (AAP), about 4.6 million children under the age of two fly every year, and under current Federal Aviation Administration (FAA) regulations, parents may carry a child under two on their laps at no additional cost. But is this truly the safest way to go? Especially with twins? While the AAP is calling for an end to lap travel, the FAA is still trying to figure out the safest way to travel with child-restraint seats. Therefore, the FAA and the AAP together have made the following recommendations:

- Until your children weigh at least twenty pounds, they should be placed in rear-facing child-safety seats that are properly installed.

- When your children are at least one year old and weigh between twenty and forty pounds, they should be placed in a forward-facing car seat that is labeled for airplane use.

While these recommendations sound like the safest and sanest way to travel with your twins, it means you have to pay for two additional tickets even if your twins aren't two yet. Ouch. For many, the trip then becomes too cost-prohibitive, and you're left with no choice but to cancel. However, for those not willing to give up quite yet, here are a few suggestions that may help:

1. Some airlines offer discounts for children's tickets, but here's the kicker: you must ask about it. The airlines typically don't advertise this information to the public.

2. Try to fly during off-peak hours or on less crowded flights. You'll have a much better chance of having empty seats around you, which will allow you and your family to spread out. Also, try asking for bulkhead seats. Those are the seats at the front of the rows that have more legroom and are less cramped than the others.

3. If your children *do* end up on your laps due to crowded flights or the expense of the tickets, a quick Google search on the Web will help you find a company that manufactures lap restraint systems approved by the FAA.

Another concern when traveling with two infants or toddlers is the seating arrangements. Unfortunately, on our first trip with our twins, we weren't lucky enough to learn about this little "detail" ahead of time and had to deal with some pretty angry passengers and hostile airline personnel. If you and your partner are traveling with your twins on your laps, you most likely will *not* be able to sit together. If the airplane seat configuration is three seats across, that means there are only three oxygen masks. The airlines will *not* let four people sit together when there are only three oxygen masks available. While this is actually a good thing, it still would have been nice to know about ahead of time. After learning the hard way, we solved the problem on subsequent flights by always booking the aisle seats across from one another. Not ideal, but close enough.

Tips from the Transportation Security Administration

The good news is that even with the new security regulations, you will never be asked to do anything that will take you away from your children. The Transportation Security Administration (TSA) has come up with the following tips to ease the security process for you and your family:

- Always allow for extra time to get through security.
- All children must be removed from strollers so they can be individually screened.
- Speak to your children ahead of time about the screening process and about what may happen so they won't be frightened or surprised. Let them know that even their backpacks or dolls will have to go through

the X-ray machine but will come out the other end and be returned to them.

- Tell your twins ahead of time that they may be asked to take off their shoes at the security checkpoint so they won't be scared when or if that happens. Let them know that the shoes will be returned immediately after the inspection.

- If they are old enough, remind your children not to joke about any threats such as bombs or explosives. Big no-no.

After the security checkpoint

You've finally made it through security, but that doesn't mean your problems are over. After speaking to many twin parents about their experiences with airplane travel, the best advice for having a smooth in-flight experience seems to be:

1. Start them young. Not only does this take the fear factor out of flying for your twins, but you'll be surprised at how much easier it becomes for the entire family when everyone knows what to expect.

2. Bring surprise toys. Just as your children are on the verge of a tantrum, or are about to have a boredom meltdown, pull out a surprise. The mood change is instantaneous, not to mention a godsend for your

nerves. And all the other passengers around you will thank you, too. Do remember to bring two of everything.

3. Don't forget to bring their favorite blanket or animal along. Been there, done that. Not pretty.

4. Make sure you bring along enough food and snacks. Especially now that some airlines don't serve food anymore. You'd be surprised at the mileage you can get out of cheese, goldfish crackers, or a bag of pretzels. Bagels with cream cheese were always a hit with my twins. Still are. If you're taking fruit along, consider where you're flying to. Certain places, Hawaii included, have strict agricultural regulations. If your particular flight does serve food, you can call ahead of time and reserve children's meals. While they're not the most nutritious in the world, at least your twins will be satisfied.

5. Always carry extra diapers on the plane. I repeat, *always* carry extra diapers with you at all times. And then, pack *at least* one more than you think you'll need.

6. Be sure to bring an extra change of clothes for each child. You never know when a bad case of air-sickness is going to hit . . . twice (unfortunately, I do). Or when a can of juice spills on that brand-new traveling dress.

Accidents happen all the time. Best to be prepared for them when they do.

7. Always bring along a pain reliever and/or fever reducer just in case. You may never need them, but it's nice to know you have them available in case you do. Besides, Tylenol or Advil can make even the wildest toddler sleepy, should you have to go that route.

8. If this is your first airplane trip, be prepared for possible ear pain. Airplane pressure can wreak havoc on little ones' ears—especially if it's their first time flying.

Traveling by car

Some families prefer this mode of transportation to flying just because they have more control over the journey and experience far fewer travel hassles. Plus, the reality is, if your children are over two, airline travel can become cost-prohibitive. A successful vacation by car also involves some creative planning. A good rule of thumb to go by when determining your destination: the younger your twins, the more stops you'll make. Obviously if you're planning to go a distance, you may want to break the driving into two days. Otherwise, car travel merely takes common sense. A lot of the tips for airplane travel also apply to automobiles: make sure you have plenty of food and water and a surprise bag of toys for each child. Play-Doh is always a favorite and coloring books come in handy. Don't forget the entertainment: portable DVD players, VCRs, and Gameboys have made car travel quite luxurious these days (not to mention a whole lot easier on parents!).

Tips for staying in hotels

While it may be more cost-effective to stay at Grandma's house or in your relatives' spare bedroom, oftentimes it's just too crowded to make it work—not to mention the hassle factor involved with setting up camp for two toddlers. And, no matter how gracious your in-laws, parents, or relatives may be, they've probably long forgotten about the noise, toys, and late-night shenanigans one toddler can cause—let alone two. Instead of worrying about whom you may be bothering or feeling like you're walking on eggshells during your vacation, sometimes it's easier just to stay elsewhere if cost is not an issue.

If you do choose to stay in a hotel, the following tips may make your transition from home to hotel more pleasant:

- Always bring along a few extra childproofing supplies. Outlet covers and toilet locks are easy to take along. Once you arrive, make sure to crawl around and check for any potential hazards. Your twins are going to be very curious about their temporary surroundings; make your environment as safe and secure as possible.

- Call your hotel ahead of time to see what gear you'll need to bring. This includes portable cribs, high chairs, and strollers. No sense in schlepping two of everything if the hotel can provide it instead.

- If you're renting a car and don't want to bring your own car seats, don't ever assume the rental company will have car seats available upon your arrival. Make sure to let them know *ahead of time* you need *two* car seats. Best to do this when you're making the rental reservation. One piece of advice: often the car seats available will be different from the ones you're used to. And *quite* filthy, I might add. Make sure to bring along some wipes to tidy them up before you use them. And if you're particularly picky about the types of seats you like for your twins, I suggest bringing your own along for peace of mind.

- Make sure you have food, food, and more food for the duration of your stay. That includes water and drinks as well. Minibar snacks and hotel food can get pricey, day after day. Plus, you'll be able to quickly head off any hunger meltdowns that happen along the way.

- If you're staying someplace with a pool, make sure you bring along any safety gear you need for the kids. And don't forget their bathing suits. While many parents choose to let their twins at this age go au naturel in the pool at home, remember this is a public pool. Behave accordingly.

Traveling with twin toddlers can be hard work. But good planning and realistic expectations can help to make your family vacations both fulfilling and fun. Don't let fear and the "hassle factor" stop you from enjoying the whole travel experience. I guarantee the memories and the photographs will make every minute of it worthwhile (well, *most* minutes, anyway!). Especially for your twins. Happy travels.

Eating Out: How Not to Get Kicked Out of Your Favorite Restaurant

Most of us associate eating out with good times, good food, and good memories. In some families, going out to eat is a way to celebrate birthdays, anniversaries, and other special occasions. In other families, eating out is a weekly event to get out of the kitchen for a night. Whatever the occasion or situation, eating out (pre-twins) is usually a very pleasant experience. Unfortunately, that's all about to change. But it's not all for the worse. Your new restaurant experience is just going to be . . . well . . . different.

Changing your expectations

The single most important piece of advice I can offer for surviving the restaurant experience with twin toddlers involves an attitude adjustment. And I mean in a big way. Sometimes you may have to entirely overhaul your expectations for the evening—just to get through it. For example:

- Don't expect your night out to be relaxing just because you don't have to cook. Sometimes it can turn out to be just the opposite.

- Don't expect it to be an opportunity to catch up with your spouse, whom you haven't seen for three days. You're going to be way too busy tending to the spilled ketchup on your children's laps or the goldfish that have been ground into the carpet.

- Don't expect to be able to finish your meal in one sitting. I'm convinced doggie bags were invented just for parents of twin toddlers.

- Don't expect the night to go smoothly. And be pleasantly surprised if it does.

Believe it or not, I spoke to many parents of twin toddlers who avoided restaurants altogether during this age. They just didn't want to deal with the hassle. Fair enough. But I don't agree with doing that. Sure, it can be a hassle. And sometimes it can be more work than it's worth. But eating out is a part of everyday life. I'm a big advocate of exposing your children to events and situations that are part of your everyday lives and that will be part of *their* lives one day, too. Plus, if it's something you enjoy, you don't have to stop just because you had twins. It's all about figuring out how to make it work while keeping your sanity intact. Who knows, you might even get to the point of actually enjoying the experience. I did. But not without offending many neighboring diners and restaurant managers along the way. To this day, there are still two restaurants I haven't set foot in since my kids were toddlers. But that's a whole other story.

While most of my memories of eating out with my twin toddlers involve big messes and big tips, I still smile when I think about those times. Through many glasses of spilled juice and hot dogs thrown across the table, I actually learned to look forward to eating out with my twins, as it was *always* a new experience. Hopefully, the following restaurant survival tips will help to make your experiences both enjoyable and memorable. And at the very least, they should help you to go back to your favorite restaurant without the owner locking the doors when he sees you coming.

Survival tips for eating out

1. Be kind and courteous to your server. While it's your server's job to try and make your dining experience a pleasant one, it's not his or her job to succumb to the demands of hungry, hyper, or cranky toddlers. On top of it all, he or she is usually left to clean up the pieces (literally) after you're done. Smiles, respect, and apologies will make all the difference in the type of service you receive.

2. Bring toys, coloring books, markers, Play-Doh, and other familiar activities to keep your twins occupied while they wait for their food. This *does not* include salt shakers, ketchup bottles, bent silverware, and shredded napkins.

3. Leave a *big* tip. Especially if it's a restaurant you want to go back to.

4. Be thoughtful of your fellow diners. If one twin starts crying or has a meltdown, be sure to take him or her outside. There's nothing worse than making all the other diners miserable just because your kid is.

5. Always be prepared to leave if the evening goes south. There's nothing wrong in admitting it may not have been the *best* night to go out when your children were teething all day. At least you tried. The food will taste just as good at home.

6. Try to clean up after yourself. Obviously, this doesn't mean doing your own dishes or busing your own table. But it does mean trying to clean up all the food that got "dropped" under the table as well as picking up crayons and empty juice-box containers.

7. Some mothers recommend feeding your twins a little something before leaving for the restaurant. That way,

your kids won't be as hungry or grouchy while waiting for their food. And it makes for a calmer dining experience overall.

8. If possible, make sure there are two adults present. While this can't always be the case, having two grown-ups available actually allows you some time to eat your own dinner. That's quite an accomplishment when you're dining with twin toddlers.

9. Did I mention be kind to your waiter and leave a big tip? I can't emphasize that one enough!

While the days of eating out and lingering over good food, good conversation, and a good bottle of wine may seem like a distant memory, just remember your twins won't be toddlers forever. And don't forget: there are always babysitters.

Cryptophasia, aka Twin Language—Does It Really Exist?

Whether it's called cryptophasia, idioglossia, autonomous language, or plain ol' twin talk, the secret language among twins has long been a source of fascination to both parents and researchers alike. According to twin statistics, about 40 percent of multiples develop some type of language between them that only they can understand. The genesis of this secret language is often quite innocent. Because twins are acquiring language at the same time, they tend to share and model what they learn with and for each other. Through this sharing, the words can grow more and more distorted, until they become unintelligible to everyone but the twins. Sometimes it involves leaving the beginning or ending sounds off words.

It can also include made-up words and nonverbal communication, as well as new sound combinations. According to Eileen M. Pearlman, PhD, director of Twinsight, cryptophasia can often last until kindergarten. She explains this secret language as "an inability to articulate properly, so the sounds that are spoken are like that of an unknown language."

While the statistics show that twin language is most likely to occur with identical twins, several moms of fraternal twins interviewed for this book report witnessing this unique communication among their own twins. It can begin quite early. Angela M. has thirteen-month-old fraternal girls. She says she sees them babbling to each other all the time and they both seem to understand and respond to the babble. Kim R. has eighteen-month-old boy/girl twins. She says she will often sneak up on her twins when they aren't looking. When one twin finally notices her, he will say something to the other that she doesn't understand and then both will turn to look at her. Sue L. remembers her identical twin boys had a secret language from about age one to two and a half. While it sounded like complete gibberish to Sue, the boys would say these words only to each other and then laugh hysterically.

Most parents take great delight in witnessing this interaction between their twins. It reminds parents of the unique intimacy and special bond their twins share. Simply by the amount of time twins spend together, they will continue to model each other's language and reinforce each other's "babble" as they grow older. Just make sure your twins learn to develop the proper language skills needed to communicate with others. While this special language can be fascinating to both the twins and their families, it can also contribute to slower language development in your children. If you find this happening with your twins, it may be helpful to follow some of the suggestions listed in the second half of Age One to aid in the language development of your pair. Always make sure to discuss any concerns with your pediatrician to see if further evaluation is necessary.

AGE 4

Out of Control, Out of Bounds

Congratulations again. You've reached your very own developmental milestone. You've been through some of the hardest years of raising twins and you've lived to tell the tale. Time to take a deep breath and pat yourself on the back for a job well done. The first several years with twins are often a blur to those of us using hindsight—but *you* are still close enough to it right now to really see how far your family has come. If you can, take a moment to think about the silly times, the frustrating tirades, the loving cuddles, and the Kodak moments before they all become distant memories and then a blur. Record your thoughts in a book. Make that photo album you've been putting off. Watch the video you made two years ago and haven't had time to watch. All too soon you'll realize how fast they grow and how easy it is to forget the delicious details you so desperately want to keep in your mind forever. Reflection is also a good time to count your blessings. Even during the toughest moments with my own twins, all it took was one smile (OK, *two*) to make me smile. And that's still the way it is. Sometimes I feel like the luckiest mom around—till adolescence, that is. (Then I reserve the right to re-evaluate.)

The good news is that by now, your twins have probably learned to eat, sleep, talk, walk, and go to the bathroom on their own. That means your life should be quite a bit easier these days. If either of your twins seems to be a bit challenged in any of those areas due to prematurity, that's OK, too. A quick trip to the pediatrician will probably confirm the "I'll get to where I'm supposed to be in my own sweet time, thank you very much!" theory. As you read earlier, it's not uncommon for twins to reach some of their milestones a bit later than their singleton buddies. That's one of the best things about age four: it's often a "catching up" age, especially for boys.

The typical four-year-old: the good, the bad, and the ugly

Your twins have reached an age where they seem to be ready for anything. The typical four-year-old loves adventure, excitement, and anything new. Children at this age are becoming more intuitive and imaginative, and love to express their feelings. Generally delighted with themselves all the time, they're quick to tell you just *how* delighted they are. If you haven't already noticed, four-year-olds have a tendency to boast and exaggerate—*all* the time. Try to take it all in stride; this type of behavior is typical. More annoying than the boasting, however, is the bad language your four-year-olds may be using right now. And I don't mean just potty talk. We're talking outright profanity. *Hell, shit, fuck, Jesus Christ,* and *God damn it* are a few that I remember hearing in my house. Boy, it was a real treat. And wait, here's the kicker: there's nothing more unnerving than hearing your four-year-old curse up a storm—only to have his or her twin sibling repeat *every word*. This is the time for you and your partner to be ultracautious about what comes out of your own mouths. Even when you don't think your twins are listening. Remember, your twins are like sponges right now. The next time someone cuts you off in traffic or you're having a little argument on the telephone, try to keep your language in check. Otherwise, you'll be hearing a repeat performance, in stereo, when you least expect it. And that's another point: it's one thing to hear this profanity coming out of their mouths at home. But it can be downright embarrassing when your twins let loose in public. While your best response is to discourage this behavior, try not to make too much of a fuss over it. In fact, the less you notice or react, the less of a thrill it will be for them to try and shock you with their new vocabulary. While this type of behavior is far from charming, try not to worry too much about it. As awful as it sounds, swearing and exaggerating are the essence of four-year-old conduct. Be patient, and this too shall disappear.

Germs and illness . . . times two

Having multiples often means multiple illnesses at the same time, especially if your children are in preschool or day care. In fact, the more time your twins spend around other children, the more germs they're exposed to. While some moms I know are absolutely phobic about germs (to the point of neurotic obsession), others take it in stride. After all, you can't keep your kids in a bubble, right? The reality is that young children make terrible patients, period. Not only do they hate the symptoms, they also hate the cure. Sometimes it helps to know your child's pain threshold before deciding how sick they really are. We've all experienced the child who shrieks at every tumble while his sibling falls from the roof without a peep. Now's the time to take those differences into account when deciding how sick your child actually is. A good rule of thumb is to always err on the side of caution. Even though you may have a cry-wolf type of child, you certainly don't want to ignore his complaints if he is indeed truly sick. Your patience may be stretched a little thin by all the complaining, but nobody likes to see their children suffer.

At this stage of the game, you've probably already experienced shared illnesses between your twins and have learned a few tools of survival along the way. Let me add to the list:

- Wash your hands and your children's hands as much as possible, especially if they've been around sick kids (and/or adults). If you're out and about and can't get to a sink, try using an antibacterial instant hand sanitizer like Purell. Keep one in your purse and one in your car.

- Know your children's health history before you call the doctor. This includes chronic medical conditions, allergies, drug reactions, and current medications. The more informed your doctor is, the better able he or she is to help your children.

- Always make sure to keep a well-stocked medicine cabinet. This includes a fever reducer, a decongestant, and something for an upset tummy. And don't forget any prescription medications your children may also be taking.

- Know where the closest twenty-four-hour pharmacy is—preferably one that delivers. For some reason, sick children seem to be at their worst in the middle of the night. Planning ahead will provide you with peace of mind if and when you actually need that information.

- Follow through with your twins' immunizations. While I know this topic is very controversial these days, make sure to discuss your concerns with your pediatrician if you don't feel that immunizations are necessary. It wasn't that long ago when getting through childhood was tricky business due to deadly and disabling infectious diseases. But thanks to immunizations, most of those diseases are extremely rare in developed countries these days. Obviously, the choice to immunize your children is yours and is very much a personal decision to be made between you and your physician. Just make sure it's an informed one.

- If one or both of your twins is sick, try not to stress about the amount of time you have to take off work. Now's the time to focus on your child's health—*not* the next client presentation you need to prepare. Believe me, your children need you far more than your work does. Work will always be there when you get back. Besides, that extra day spent with an ill child may be just what the doctor ordered—for both of you.

- If only one twin is sick and you're taking him or her to the doctor, you may want to take the other twin, too. Your pediatrician may be able to see early signs of the same illness developing and will be able to treat it accordingly. It certainly can't hurt and it just may save you another trip.

- Some twins will pretend to be sick just for the attention. If the healthy twin sees how much attention the sick twin is getting, he or she may suddenly feel sick, too. Know when you're being played and when to take your child seriously. Either way, always make sure to give plenty of TLC to both.

- Certain illnesses are harder to handle than others. If you haven't experienced it yet, let me be the first to warn you that there's nothing worse than the stomach flu, times two. While I don't have any great pearls of wisdom for getting through this one, the best advice is to try to have another adult around for the duration of the illness. Be prepared to do lots of extra laundry and extra cleaning. Expect your twins to be more clingy than normal and to want to be close to you—all the time. Every time my daughter got the stomach flu, two things always happened: first, she *always* got sick in the middle of the night. I don't remembering ever having the luxury of daylight to deal with this messy malady. Second, she always rushed into my bed at the *exact* moment she had to throw up. Not the toilet, not the sink, but my *bed*. You can imagine my delight at waking up at two in the morning to find fresh vomit in my bed, often on my pillow. To this day, we laugh about her inability to make it anywhere but my bed when the urge hit her. While it's funny in hindsight, believe me, there was no humor in it *at all* when it was happening. Time does wonderful things to bad memories.

- Continue to expect many shared illnesses between your twins. While the preschool years tend to be the worst, shared illnesses continue even as your children get older—though not necessarily at the same time. Just another component of the multiple experience.

Your twins have their own preferences now

At this age, it's common for parents to see many distinctions emerging between their twins. One may begin to shine as an athlete while the other shows great promise at creative pursuits. Accepting your twins for who they are and who they are becoming is especially important right now. One or both of your twins may put undue pressure on themselves to keep up with the other. Now's the time to praise their individual accomplishments and let them know that it's OK to be different from their twin by not doing everything the same way or at the same time. You may even notice a big difference in their temperaments, too. A quiet, shy, mild-mannered child may exhibit more boisterous, lively, and out-of-bounds behavior, which may be completely out of character for him or her. Not to worry. These new characteristics are hallmarks of four-year-old behavior. It's their time to test the limits and see how far they can push. Just make sure to have very distinct boundaries set in place. Most four-year-olds love to know what the rules are even though they "occasionally" like to break them, too. The best advice I can give you is to make sure to give your twins considerable leeway during this time and recognize that they probably won't accomplish new skills at exactly the same moment. Enjoy observing their emerging talents and temperaments, and be ready for anything.

Unpredictable, egocentric, noisy, enthusiastic, amusing . . .

And the list goes on to describe this age. Their self-expression, imagination, and versatility are truly expansive right now. Try not to be too bothered by some of the unacceptable behavior your twins may exhibit. Obviously, safety is foremost when either twin goes out of bounds. In fact, they desperately need boundaries at this age and are typically very responsive to those provided. Four-year-olds are also very responsive to praise and compliments. No amount of compliments seems to be too much for your little egocentrics' insatiable appetites. Silliness and silly language are other ways to motivate or restrain. Made-up, funny-sounding words seem to work wonders. Your twins are also at an age when bargaining can be effective. They're old enough now to understand the give-and-take involved in working out a problem, and most are willing to indulge you, if necessary. As with any age, try to accept your twins for who they are. All too quickly you'll find your overexuberant four-year-olds turning into conforming five-year-olds. And before you know it, they're off to kindergarten. Enjoy these early years while you can; they'll be over in a blink. (Big sigh.)

Learning to Tame Your Two Devils

From cursing to imaginary companions to preschool, your four-year-olds are both stormy and stunning at the same time. And always on the go. Their fascination with bowel movements, body parts, and bad language can exasperate even the most tolerant parent—on a daily basis. One child going through this stage is taxing enough. Two going through it can make four padded walls and a straitjacket look unusually appealing. The irony of this age is that on some days, you may find yourself completely fascinated with how your twins are flourishing. It can be amazing to watch the differences emerge between your twins and to observe how they each go about improving and perfecting their skills. But on the other overwhelming days, when all you want to do is crawl back into bed, pull the covers over your head, and wait for this wild ride to be over, just remember: *it's not you.* Keep reminding yourself that this is just a stage and that their behavior is completely age-appropriate. If you can remember this, it will help you to understand and appreciate your twin's age-related "self-expression" —instead of feeling angry and overwhelmed about it. The real question now becomes how to handle them and still get through your day. Before we get to that, though, let's talk about some of the issues you may have to deal with along the way.

Imagination and fantasy life

During this age your children's imaginations are taking off. There tends to be lots of dress-up during playtime and you may witness your twins becoming more imaginative with their toys and playmates. Generally speaking, fantasy helps children understand the world around them. Some children may use dramatic play to relive and try to understand certain experiences that were emotionally important to them. This is also the time when your children's imaginations help them to be, or create, anyone they want. Many imaginary friends are born around this time. My twins actually created a mutual imaginary friend named Jackson. He pretty much went with us everywhere we went. Often he was "surfing" on top of the car, or "flying" right next to us. In fact, he became such a big part of our lives during this time that when he wasn't "with" us, I would casually ask my kids where he was. They took great delight in my playing along with the fantasy. Plus, my involvement with Jackson made them feel comfortable and secure in sharing that part of their lives with me. Over the next several months, Jackson gradually disappeared from our lives. But to this day, we still laugh about our long-lost friend Jackson and jokingly wonder where he might be or what he might be doing. While my kids were very open with me about Jackson, other kids might not be as willing to share their fantasy friends. If that's the case, try to respect their privacy, as they may feel like you're "trespassing" in their territory. If you have a "Jackson" in your lives, don't worry. This behavior is completely normal. This imaginary friend will most likely disappear from your lives as quickly as it appeared as your children develop more social skills. And if your family is like mine, you'll have lots of fun memories to reminisce about for many years to come. Imaginary play should always be encouraged and respected. Through imagination, children are able to develop empathy and a sense of humor, and to assimilate new learning.

"Why" this, "why" that?

"Why is it so hot today?" "Why is the tree so tall?" "Why is your hair blonde?" Why, why, why? If you haven't yet found yourself besieged by the why questions, just wait. As your twins move through the preschool years, they're more capable of imagining a broader range of possibilities to the questions they ask. Often the questions are a way of getting or keeping your attention. Sometimes they're used as a way to keep you talking. The truth of the matter is, much of the time, the "why" questions are simply annoying. Especially when they're coming at you in stereo. If you can, answer the questions as briefly as possible. Or, turn the question around and ask your little inquisitor to talk a little bit more about what she's interested in learning about. When you're asked a truly unanswerable question (more often than not), you can offer to help look for the answer online or at the library if you have the time or inclination. There's no doubt that receiving a double dose of "whys" can be trying on your nerves. Answer the best you can and know that this phase, like all others, shall pass as quickly as it came.

Aggression

Between the ages of three and six, children begin to express aggression differently. They are less likely to fight physically and more likely to use threats, teasing, and insults. Some children "act out" on other children the stresses they are feeling at home. Aggressive behavior is often a way to gain attention. If one twin feels he isn't getting the same amount of attention at home as his twin sibling, he may act more aggressively at school. This is the time to focus on using positive reinforcement and praise when your child exhibits good behavior. It's up to you to teach your twins the difference between good and bad behavior. All preschoolers need help with curbing aggressive tendencies and understanding why it's not OK to yell, hit, or push other children. You may find yourself repeating the familiar mantra "Use your words, not your hands" many times throughout the day. If you're like most parents of twins, you'll be using this phrase a lot longer than parents of singletons do. Because of their twinship, your children have had to worry about "ownership" pretty much since the day they were born. If one twin snatched a favorite toy away from the other, she learned the lesson earlier than most that she must learn to control her anger and tolerate frustration when she can't do or get what she wants. In order to be accepted socially, *all* children must learn to control aggression and to consider the desires and feeling of others. Not surprisingly, many studies suggest that boys are more aggressive than girls. Parents of twin boys need to be extra vigilant when it comes to helping their children learn how to control their aggressive tendencies.

One thing to be aware of is that children crave attention, good *or* bad, and will do most anything to get it. While most children would rather have good attention than bad, bad attention is better than no attention. I can't tell you the number of times I would be doing something with one twin only to have the other twin throw a tantrum for no apparent reason. When a child realizes he can get your attention by acting a certain way (i.e., naughty), he may think the attention is worth the trouble. It's up to you to let your child know why this isn't OK and to explain what type of behavior you expect from him. Discuss the consequences of his behavior and suggest other ways for him to handle his frustrations. Over time, children begin to understand what kinds of behaviors are expected of them and eventually learn that the most effective way to resolve conflicts is to share, take turns, and play cooperatively with others.

Fears

Every child has her own fears and worries, but certain anxieties are more prevalent during the preschool years. One reason may be children's highly active imaginations. Disasters, real or imagined, become particularly worrisome to this age group—especially if they hear something bad on the radio or TV. Plane crashes, natural disasters, and getting lost are fairly common fears of this age. Most children also feel anxious about getting hurt. If you haven't done so already, now's the time to stock up on potential "feel better" aids: Band-Aids, ice packs, "boo-boo friends" (animal-shaped ice packs or heating pads), Neosporin, or whatever you use to make your twins' "owies" feel better. You can pretty much count on having to tend to every bump, bruise, scratch, and skinned knee, no matter how serious. And don't ever underestimate the healing power of a single Band-Aid. You'd be amazed at how the pain instantly disappears once the "injury" is covered. Speaking of pain, your preschoolers may dread their next visit to the pediatrician in anticipation of any shots they may have to get. This focus on potential pain is normal at this age. The best way to handle your twins' fears is to be reassuring. Let them know that their safety is still your responsibility and that you are there for them no matter what. If possible, try to anticipate things that are likely to bother each child, without being overprotective. Never tease a child or downplay his or her fears; this will only encourage the child to hide fears while pretending to be brave. Make sure your twins know that teasing one another about their fears can be cruel and hurtful. Don't be surprised if the fears one child experiences become contagious. One twin may become fearful of something just because the other is. On that note, make sure to keep an excess supply of Band-Aids handy; "sympathy" pain can hurt just as much as the real thing. As your children's coping skills evolve with time, they will begin to feel more safe and capable. Once this happens, many of these fears and anxieties begin to diminish.

Firm discipline is important right now

You will need to use a good deal of firmness in dealing with your twins right now. All children need rules and expectations not only to keep them safe, but to teach them the difference between right and wrong. Discipline is most effective when a child is continuously exposed to the consequences of his or her behavior. According to the American Academy of Child & Adolescent Psychiatry (AACAP), having logical consequences for misbehavior helps kids learn that they are accountable for their actions without damaging their self-esteem. While there are many different approaches to parenting, one thing is certain: consistency and predictability are the cornerstones to effective discipline. The AACAP recommends that once you and your partner establish the rules, you let your children know what the rules are and what will happen if they're broken. At the same time, offer positive reinforcement and support when the rules are followed.

Now that your twins are preschoolers, they are ready to assume some responsibility for their own safety and security. Keep in mind that what works for one child may not work for the other. One twin may respond to having a privilege taken away, while the other responds to a time-out. Speaking of time-outs, be careful how you handle them if your twins share a room. If they do, sending one of them to their room for a time-out may actually seem like a reward instead of a consequence. Try to find a neutral place in your house where you can at least split them up. In our house, we never found time-outs to be very effective, especially if both twins got them. There would be constant arguments about *who* got the better location. Even discipline provoked competition between my two! On the other hand, some parents swear by them. Find what works with your own two and stick with it. According to the AACAP, other tips for effective discipline include:

- Make sure what you ask for is reasonable.

- Model positive behavior. The "do as I say, not as I do" approach seldom works.

- Be clear about what you mean by being firm and specific.

- Make sure the consequences are fair and appropriate—not only to the situation but to your children's age and stage of development.

- Try to make sure the consequences are delivered immediately and directly relate to the rule that has been broken.

- Allow for flexibility when warranted.

This is the age when your twins are expected to learn behavior that will help them to enter the world beyond you and your family. Effective discipline will help them come to terms with the many expectations society has for them. It also teaches them self-control. Learning self-discipline takes time. Always take the time to explain *why* something is wrong or why they must act a certain way. And try not to criticize. Children respond best when they're shown correct behavior, not when they're criticized for bad behavior.

When you're being tag-teamed by two, sometimes one of the most difficult things is to keep your own cool, especially if you suspect one or the other is deliberately trying to provoke or annoy you. This is normal. If you feel yourself getting angrier than you'd like, sometimes it helps to physically step away from the situation, if that's at all possible. Not only will this give you some breathing room to try to calm yourself down, but you'll be able to gain some emotional perspective, as well. In addition, always be ready to apologize if you make a mistake. This shows you have consideration for your children's feelings and models the kind of behavior you'd like them to emulate. Studies suggest that a parenting style combining emotional warmth with firmness works best for teaching a range of values. Remember, it's your job to provide your twins with the basics for appropriate and responsible social behavior.

COMIC RELIEF FROM THE TRENCHES . . .

"*And,* She Will Be . . ."

Meghan B. has four-year-old fraternal boys. One day, the family was having a conversation about marriage. Meghan turned to her boys and jokingly said, "So, guys, who do you want to marry when you grow up?" One twin innocently responded, "I want to marry my twin brother." Everyone chuckled. The other twin then gave a description of the woman *he* wanted to marry: "She will be beautiful, she will listen to me, and she will *not* be crazy." There's a kid who knows what he wants.

AGE 5

Devils Turned Angels

What an endearing age. While four-year-olds are continually testing themselves, five-year-olds tend to be much more secure and well adjusted. That's good news, because big changes are on the horizon. The jump from preschool to kindergarten is monumental and will once again require some important decision-making. You'll read much more about that in the second half of this chapter. In the meantime, let's take a peek at what you can expect from your two little "angels."

Happy and content

Enjoy this time with your twins right now; you won't experience such an equilibrium again until your twins turn ten. That's not to say the years in between are horrible and tumultuous (well, some *can* be). It's just that right now, moms are the center of their twins' universe (sorry, dads). Who can resist such admiration, especially when it's multiplied by two? Five-year-olds tend to be reliable and stable, and quite content to live in the here and now. They like to be near Mom and are happy to do things with her and for her. Additionally, their goal to obey and please Mom is almost always accomplished. While that may sound like you've hit the jackpot, just remember you've got two vying for your attention at once. Be aware of any jealousy that may arise when either twin feels as though their attention is not being reciprocated. Since you are the sole focus of their lives right now, having to share you may cause some bickering. As of yet, none of us have figured out how to split ourselves in two, so do try to spend some alone time with each. This way, each twin has the opportunity to "please" you on his own and demonstrate how "good" he can be in your presence.

School readiness

Just like you did before preschool, it's time again to take a look at your twins and gather the information needed to make an accurate decision about whether they're ready for school. The following list from the AACAP gives you an overview of some general indicators of school readiness:

- Physical health and well-being
- Motor development: drawing, using scissors, running, jumping, climbing
- Social competence and emotional well-being: self-esteem and confidence
- Approach to learning—curiosity, ability to work independently, persistence, listening skills, pride in job well done
- Language skills
- General knowledge of the world around him or her

Additionally, according to the American Academy of Pediatrics, the following skills will help make your children's kindergarten year go more smoothly:

- Playing well with other children with minimal fighting or crying
- Remaining attentive and quiet when being read a story
- Being able to use the toilet on their own
- Successfully using zippers and buttons

- Being able to say their name, address, and telephone number

With many sets of twins, there are large differences in the maturity level of each child—which may make your decision a bit more complicated. Besides the factors listed above, other factors for parents of twins to consider include the sex of the twins, month of birth, and any lasting effects from a premature birth. Any one of these factors can contribute to your children's maturity, or lack thereof. That can make it especially complicated to decide if *both* twins are ready to be enrolled at the same time. A few things to keep in mind when evaluating your twins:

- Girls tend to mature earlier than boys.

- Identicals may be more dependent on each other than fraternals at an early age (although my *fraternal* twins were incredibly dependent on one another at this age . . .).

- Be aware of complications from a premature birth resulting in delayed language development, problems with motor control, or any other health issues associated with it.

Obviously, the best-case scenario would be to have your twins start their schooling together. But for some sets of multiples, that may not be an option. If you're faced with the difficult decision that one should start kindergarten while the other remains behind in preschool another year, don't despair. Like everything else with twins, there is no one solution that fits all. Consider all the factors involved and enlist outside help if you need to. Professional help from the medical community and/or school personnel may help you to make a more informed decision. And don't forget about other parents of twins. I often found them to offer the best advice and support of all.

If you're looking for tools to help your children with this new transition, books are always helpful. While I can't personally endorse the following books, which target this age group, they come highly recommended from other moms in the same boat: *Timothy Goes to School* by Rosemary Wells and *The Kissing Hand* by Audrey Penn.

Don't be surprised at the strength of the emotions you may be feeling right now. Starting kindergarten is often a bittersweet time, and sending two together at once only compounds your feelings about it. Take a deep breath and try to relax. On the heels of this decision comes one of the hardest decisions of all: classroom placement together or apart. You'll learn everything you need to know about making that decision in the second half of this chapter.

Establishing healthy habits

Nutrition

It's never too early to help your twins develop healthy lifestyle habits to support their well-being for many years to come. Good nutrition and exercise are crucial to healthy lives. While good nutritional habits actually began when your twins were infants, it's up to you to reinforce these good habits throughout each new stage of your kids' lives. With childhood obesity on the rise, it's more important than ever to help your kids make healthy choices. Results from a 1999–2002 National Health and Nutrition Examination Survey (NHANES) using measured heights and weights indicated that an estimated 16 percent of children ages 6 to 19 are overweight. This represents a 45 percent increase from the overweight estimates of 11 percent obtained from the NHANES survey from 1988–1994. More specifically, here are some statistics from the American Heart Association on overweight children in the U.S.:

Percentage of Overweight American Children Age 6–11

	BOYS	**GIRLS**
WHITE	11.9 %	12 %
AFRICAN AMERICAN	17.6 %	22.1 %
HISPANIC	27.3 %	19.6 %

Percentage of Overweight American Teens Age 12–19		
	BOYS	**GIRLS**
WHITE	13 %	12.2 %
AFRICAN AMERICAN	20.5 %	25.7 %
HISPANIC	27.5 %	19.4 %

Remember, kids learn by example. If they see you making healthy food choices, they're more likely to follow in your footsteps. The American Heart Association has published *Dietary Recommendations for Children and Adolescents: A Guide for Practitioners*, which focuses on healthy eating behaviors. The following key recommendations for children two and older have been endorsed by the American Academy of Pediatrics:

- Balance dietary calories with physical activity to maintain normal growth.
- Get sixty minutes of moderate to vigorous physical activity daily.
- Eat vegetables and fruits daily, and limit juice intake.

- Use vegetable oils and soft margarines low in saturated fat and trans fatty acids instead of butter or most other animal fats.

- Eat whole-grain breads and cereals rather than refined grain products.

- Reduce the intake of sugar-sweetened beverages and foods.

- Use nonfat or low-fat milk and dairy products daily.

- Eat more fish, especially oily fish, broiled or baked.

- Reduce salt intake, including salt from processed foods.

Obviously, at this age, the idea is not to count calories. Establishing healthy habits when your children are young helps to prevent the development of risk factors that can lead to obesity, heart disease, and stroke. Plus, you want to make sure your children are meeting their nutritional needs. Consuming too many calories on extra fat and sugar not only leads to excess weight gain, it doesn't allow your children to meet their nutritional requirements. Moderation is important. Eating healthy doesn't mean you can't ever satisfy a sweet tooth. If your children are eating healthy meals, it's OK to offer them ice cream for dessert. The way I look at it, you don't want them to feel deprived. That may lead to unhealthy weight issues down the road. Plus, if they're not getting their sweet tooth satisfied in your own home, you can bet they'll be feasting on junk food in someone else's. My daughter had a friend named Kaylee whose mom was incredibly strict about what she allowed her to eat. No sweets, no chips, no juice, no junk, no nothing. Whenever Kaylee came over to our house for a playdate, she practically went on a feeding frenzy. It got to the point where I had to step in and restrict the amount of junk food she consumed at my house. Providing a balanced diet will help to eliminate the need to go nuts over any one particular food group.

At this age, there are many fun ways to help your children learn how to make healthy choices. One of the easiest is to let your children cook with you. Most kids love to putter around in the kitchen at this age. Getting your twins involved will give them a hands-on lesson in the preparation of healthy foods. But beware: a trio in your kitchen can sometimes be more work than it's worth. If three together is too much to handle (and it usually is for most), have your twins help out one at a time. Not only will this solve the problem of who gets to pour the ingredients into which bowl, it allows your twins to have a one-on-one experience with you.

Despite your best efforts, many children of this age can continue to be picky eaters. That was certainly the case in my household. When either of my kids began to complain about a dinner, I insisted they try at least one bite. That way, they couldn't get away with judging the food based on color, shape, or texture alone. Sometimes it worked, sometimes it didn't. On the nights that it didn't work, I tried to make sure I enforced the "the kitchen is closed for the night" rule. While I was happy to help them get a healthy snack (so they wouldn't complain that I was starving them to death), I was *not* going to cook a second dinner. My theory is that children will eat when they're hungry enough. If they know ahead of time that you're not going to indulge their needs by cooking them something different, they'll make more of an effort to eat what you make. Sometimes this takes a little creativity. Many times I turned to animal-shaped cookie cutters to entice my kids to try something new. This seemed to do the trick for sandwiches, quesadillas, casseroles, and even hamburger meat. Some stores actually sell precooked chicken tenders in fun shapes. This became a weekly staple in our house. When it came to vegetables, I always made sure to have tasty dips available to try out. Ranch dressing and peanut butter became two of our favorites. Once you find something that works with your kids, stick with it, as long as it's healthy. While *you* may be bothered by the lack of variety, your kids probably aren't. As they get older, though, you'll probably have to modify things a bit. My daughter developed a very sophisticated palate along the way and I wasn't able to get away with the same things after a while. Now she's a vegetarian and loves to create her own meals. A few reminders: if your children skip a meal, it's not the end of the world. Like adults, children go through times when they're just not hungry, period. Unless it becomes a habit, don't worry about it. They'll most likely make up for it throughout the day. Also, try to make an effort to prepare things that you know your children will like. While I'm all for introducing new foods into their diets, there's no sense in setting yourself up for failure every night by insisting they try something new. Maybe have one or two nights a week as your "experiment" nights. If the new meal is a flop, don't despair. Kids are fickle. What didn't work today may become their favorite down the road.

Do keep in mind that kids take their cues from their parents when it comes to food issues. If you insist upon following the "clean your plate" rule, your children will, too. And with the oversized food portions served in today's society, following the "clean your plate" rule may be setting your twins up for some problems down the road.

Exercise

Exercise is also vitally important to your children's health, and it's never too early to get them started. Physical activity strengthens muscles, bones, and joints and gives children the opportunity to gain self-esteem, confidence, and a sense of well-being. And with the stats you read earlier about the rise of childhood obesity, being couch potatoes is not an option.

Physical inactivity can become a serious problem for many children. For one thing, inactive children are likely to become inactive adults. According to a 2000 study, *Media in the Home: The Fifth Annual Survey of Parents and Children,* the average child spends up to six hours watching television, playing video games, and surfing the Internet each day. The CDC recommends making physical activity part of the daily routine by:

1. Becoming a physically active role model.

2. Adding physical activity, such as hiking, biking, or long walks, to weekend or vacation plans.

3. Encouraging children to participate in sixty minutes of moderate to vigorous physical activity per day.

4. Finding fun, physically active ways to celebrate special occasions such as swimming or roller-skating birthday parties.

5. Making sure you and your family walk at every available opportunity.

6. Taking the time to be physically active with your children by playing tennis, bike riding, playing handball, playing catch, or dancing to your favorite music together.

For many parents, it's not unusual to hear "I'm bored" two minutes into an activity. This is the time to use your creativity to liven up whatever activity you are involved in. And with two, that's much easier to do. When taking a hike or an outdoor stroll, see who can collect the most leaves or rocks. Or who can count the most birds. Up the stakes with a reward such as a sticker or a bottle of bubbles. A bottle of bubbles can lead to hours of playtime outside. Other ideas include:

- Taking turns walking the dog.
- Spending time at the neighborhood playground.
- Turning your walk or hike into a scavenger hunt: who can find a worm, a blue house, a grasshopper, etc.
- Walking backwards, hopping on one leg, running to the next tree.
- Emphasizing numbers and counting: How many houses are there on this block? How many cats have we seen? How many steps to get to the next tree?

I must admit, living in Southern California, we're spoiled by our good weather. My kids essentially live outside 24/7. For those of you who aren't blessed with year-round sunshine, there are plenty of fun things to organize indoors, as well. Tumbling classes and karate classes are usually a favorite among this age group. At home you can easily set up a child-friendly obstacle course, have a freeze-dance contest, or set up a simple, *friendly* contest between your twins: who can do the most somersaults, or who can skip around the house or jump rope the longest. You get the idea. While many parents may be eager to enroll their children in organized sports at this age, you may want to wait until your twins acquire the attention span, skills, and coordination needed to play sports. You'll have plenty of time for that later. If you do choose to join a team, just make sure the emphasis at this age is on learning the basics—like running in the right direction, following the rules, and taking turns.

Big-Kid School—Together or Apart?

Talk about a loaded question. Just about everyone seems to have a different theory on whether or not to separate twins into different classrooms when they start kindergarten. Believe it or not, some of these theories seem to have changed even since *my* twins were in kindergarten—just five years ago. It used to be *never* separate, then it became *always* separate, and now it's fallen somewhere in the middle: sometimes together, sometimes apart, depending on the individual needs of the twins. What's a parent to do? Let me start by saying there's no right or wrong answer. And while that doesn't make your decision any easier, the best answer is to do what *you* think is best for your twins. You know them better than anyone—which makes you the most qualified person to make that decision based on individual needs, personalities, and opportunities. This is not a decision for the school principal, or the kindergarten teachers, or the school counselor to make (although you will need to work with them to meet the individual needs of your twins). This is your decision, period. That's not to say everyone else in your life isn't going to have an opinion about it. Aunt Sally's going to tell you about her neighbor's twins who were traumatized for life by being separated too early. Then there were your husband's law partner's identical nieces who were *not* separated but decided not to talk to anyone but each other (including the teacher) for the duration of kindergarten. You're going to be inundated with stories, each with a different outcome. You're even going to come across certain schools that have policies requiring twins to be separated. I don't know about you, but I've never been very good at being told what to do. You can imagine my reaction to some stodgy old school administrator telling *me*, good ol' Mom, what's best for *my* children. If you find yourself in a similar scenario, don't fret. Let's take a look at the advantages and disadvantages of separate classroom placement as well as what the latest research shows, to help make your decision just a little bit easier.

Keeping your twins together in school

After much consternation, you've decided to keep your twins together to begin kindergarten. Your twins have not spent a great deal of time apart and remain dependent on each other. These are two good indicators that you should not split them up yet. According to *Placement of Multiple Birth Children in School*, a publication from the National Organization of Mothers of Twins Clubs, other valid reasons for your decision include:

- Your twins want to be together. At this age, young children often feel more secure about separating from you if they're together with their twin. Especially if they haven't had a lot of exposure to other playmates.

- There's turbulence on the home front. Any type of major upheaval at home is also a good reason to keep your twins together at school. Death, divorce, even a move are emotionally traumatic events at any age. Allow your twins the comfort and support of being with each other at school.

- Only one classroom is available at the school you've chosen. A no-brainer.

- You're concerned about unequal educations due to different teachers and teaching methods. While there is a lesson to be learned about the value of having to adapt to individual differences, you or your twins may not be quite ready for that. Do what you feel most comfortable doing right now.

- One twin has a one-sided dependency on the other. Or, one twin has health concerns that are exacerbated by stress. Obviously, this is not the best time to separate them. Once the issues have calmed down or resolved themselves, you can reevaluate the situation and make any changes you feel are necessary.

- Your twins will have the same homework, the same field trips, and the same curriculum. Not only will this simplify your life, it will give your twins plenty of opportunities to work together both socially and academically.

Separating your twins in school

There are just as many reasons to separate your twins in school as there are to keep them together. Again, it comes down to the individual needs of your twins. Consider the following:

- Your twins are distracted by each other in the classroom, which is inhibiting their ability to get their work done or is causing disruptive behavior. This is a good indicator that your twins will do much better apart.

- Classmates and/or teachers are constantly comparing your twins, to the detriment of the less talented or the less popular twin. This is an unhealthy situation for any child. Nip it in the bud immediately and separate them as quickly as possible.

- Your twins do not want to be together. While ultimately this is your decision to make, it's always a good idea to take into account what your twins want.

- Your twins have very different needs and skills. And the

only way to meet their individual needs is through different classrooms.

- The constant togetherness is hindering the development of social skills of one or both of the twins. Separating them allows them to grow individually and to make their own friends.

- One twin is completely overshadowed by the other socially, physically, and academically. It's never a good idea to have your twins together in a place where one is constantly overshadowing the other. Separating them allows each to develop their own strengths without direct comparison. It's easier on everybody.

- Your twins continually exploit their relationship by playing tricks. While this may seem humorous in the short term, teachers and troublemakers don't mix well in the long term. Separate and set them straight.

You can always change your mind

Still confused? It's not uncommon for parents of twins to consider all the variables and still not be able to make a decision. One expert recommends that if you're still unsure about what to do, let the twins stay together. This allows them to gradually separate on their own timetable. And don't worry about making the wrong decision at first. I did and my kids let me know it.

When my twins were in their last year of preschool, I decided to try to separate them. Evan was put in the "Yellow" room and Maya was put in the "Purple" room. The rooms were right next to each other with a door in between. Several times a day, Evan would get up in the middle of a lesson plan and go sit in his sister's room. He'd then get involved in her classroom activities as if they were his own and forget all about his own classroom. It wasn't until the Yellow room teacher came next door, tapped him on the shoulder, and told him to come back to his own room that he realized he was in the wrong room. After several weeks of this back and forth behavior, the teachers and I decided the separation was not working and switched him into the Purple room to be with his sister. In retrospect, I was lucky both teachers were so easygoing about letting Evan feel out his comfort zone. They reacted quickly and professionally to Evan's needs as well as to my own changing needs. While I knew it would ultimately be best for my twins to separate at some point, obviously this wasn't the right time. Plus, I was pretty flexible about the timing of it all. I wanted it to happen when they were *both* ready and I certainly didn't want to put any undue emotional stress on either of them by separating them too soon. Evan's constant worry about his absent twin was glaring evidence that he wasn't ready. We were lucky we were able to remedy the situation as quickly as we did.

This highlights the importance of recognizing that all twins have their own unique dynamics and developmental timetables. Placement in separate classrooms does not fit the needs of all twins any more than placement together does. Your decision about classroom placement must be one that supports your twins' relationship and individual development. And it's a decision that has an important effect on their relationship and overall well-being.

Since our "failed separation attempt" in preschool, I've learned that many twins who start preschool together actually make a better adjustment both academically and socially later on than those who are separated. Most are just not ready to separate from you *and* their lifelong companion. But once they've adjusted to school, separating them later (in kindergarten or first grade) happens much more naturally and easily. That certainly was the case for Maya and Evan. Putting them back together that year was the smartest thing I could have done. By kindergarten, they felt safe and secure enough to separate from one another and both flourished on their own in different classrooms.

Try to remain flexible

The key to a successful decision is to remain flexible. As I learned through my preschool experience, not everything is going to go the way you think it will. Your vision of what you want for your twins or what you think your twins need must be continually reevaluated throughout these next few years. Maybe your twins started kindergarten together, but by the end of the year their teacher recommended separation. While you may not agree, keep an open mind. Their teacher may have some valuable insights into their relationship at school that you may not witness at home. After hearing the teacher's input, speak to your children to find out about their own thoughts and feelings. You may be surprised by what you hear. Once you have all the data, you can make a well-informed decision. Just make sure your decision is not influenced by any internal school policy on twins. Many schools, principals, and teachers still believe that twins should be separated in classrooms. In a 1989 NOMOTC study, teachers believed that separation promoted a positive self-concept as well as intellectual growth. Ironically, ten years later, 80 percent of teachers surveyed felt that the issue of multiples was rarely discussed in teacher-preparation programs at the college level. Result? Many teachers and school administrators are ill-prepared to make a decision about what's best for your twins without getting to know them first. Furthermore, placement decisions should not be made solely for the purpose of promoting individuality or for the teachers' convenience. Schools need to maintain a flexible placement policy because successful placement should be a collaborative decision addressing the following factors: ease of separation from the parent, ease of separation from the twin, successful academic growth, and successful social growth.

Do schools use any guidelines when making placement decisions for twins?

According to the Office of Educational Research and Improvement, there is very little research available related to this topic.

However, many organizations dedicated to the welfare of twins, as well as many parents of twins (not to mention twins themselves), believe schools should *not* have a fixed practice of separation, but a policy that encourages flexibility and decision making on a case-by-case basis. To that end, the NOMOTC's booklet *Placement of Multiple Birth Children: A Guide For Educators*, outlines basic principles that should be taken into account. If necessary, bring your school a copy of the following:

1. Schools should maintain a flexible placement policy throughout the early elementary school years.

2. Teachers at the primary, middle, and high school levels should value parental input regarding the nature of the multiples' relationship.

3. Schools should provide an atmosphere that respects the close nature of the multiple bond while at the same time encouraging individual abilities.

4. Educators should move with extreme caution when considering retention or acceleration for any child who is a multiple.

5. School districts should provide staff at all grade levels with multiple-related research and reading materials.

What the latest research shows

While most of the "to separate or not to separate" research that exists involves survey research or informal studies, twins researchers Nancy L. Segal and Jean M. Russell actually conducted a study in 1992 entitled *Twins in the Classroom: School Policy Issues and Recommendations*, published in the *Journal of Educational and Psychological Consultation*. They questioned sixty-three mothers of young twins and triplets with respect to satisfaction regarding school policies, reasons to support or reject separate classrooms, and other related issues. Not surprisingly, 35 percent of parents of identical twins favored common class placement in the early grades, while only 13 percent of parents of fraternal twins did. Also, 48 percent of the parents who were aware of the school's policy did not endorse a general practice of separating twins.

Another study, published in 2004 in England, investigated the effects of classroom separation on twins' behavior, school progress, and reading abilities. Three groups of twins were followed from age five to seven and divided into the following groups: twins who were in the same class at both ages, twins who were in separate classes at both ages, and twins who were in the same class at age five but separated at age seven. When compared to those *not* separated, the twins who separated earlier had significantly more teacher-rated problems. Those separated later showed lower reading scores. And, not surprisingly, identicals exhibited more problems as a result of separation than fraternals.

Most of the research on the effects of twin separation is still pretty limited. Much of what has been published is anecdotal or has appeared in non-peer-reviewed journals. One formal research study done in 1970 by Leeper and Skipper paired twins in grades 1 through 6 into two groups: twins who had been separated and twins who had not. While they discovered some differences occurring at certain grade levels, no reliable pattern emerged. The bottom line: there is *no* research-based rationale for separating twins or keeping them together.

More informal studies reveal similar outcomes. In an informal NOMOTC survey of fifty-eight families (88 percent with twins, 12 percent with triplets), 25 percent of parents opted for separation initially and an additional 31 percent opted for separation the following year. Almost all of those subsequent separations occurred in first grade after the children had attended kindergarten together. A relatively small percentage of families (10 percent) had no choice due to the size of the school. And only 5 percent of the families faced a rigid school policy—although they did not assume the policy, no matter how rigid, was impervious. When they really questioned the reasoning behind the rigid policies, they were able to show that there was no empirical evidence to support the claim that separation eases the competition between twins. School personnel imposed the final decision on an additional 2 percent of the families surveyed.

The bottom line

Regardless of the current research (or lack thereof), I'll go back to where I started at the beginning of this chapter: as a parent, this is *your* decision to make based on the individual needs of your twins. While it's nice to have a point of reference and read about what everyone else is doing, don't lose sight of your ultimate goal: to make a decision based on your twins' developmental needs *right now.* A successful placement is one that takes into account the separation both from you and from their twin, not to mention one that promotes successful social and academic growth. Keep in mind that nothing is written in stone. If you separated and realize you shouldn't have, or didn't separate and realize you should have, don't freak out. If you're at the right school, the personnel should be willing to work with you to rectify any mistake that was made. And don't worry about the mistake causing any lasting effects on the emotional well-being of your twins. We still laugh about Evan taking it upon himself to get to where he felt he needed to be. There's nothing like taking control of the situation at four years old! The best thing you can do for your twins is to do what feels right to you. If you change your mind tomorrow, so be it. You know them best and they're counting on you to do whatever you think is best for them *right now.*

COMIC RELIEF FROM THE TRENCHES . . .

"Oops, Wrong Twin"

Matt and Steve are six-year-old identical twins with lots of the same friends. Normally, they're both invited to the same parties, but on one occasion only Matt was invited to a very small sleepover. On the evening of the party, Dad put both kids in the car to take Matt to the party. When he got there, he dropped Steve off instead of Matt. Neither twin said anything. When Matt arrived home with his dad, his mom said to him, "Honey, what are you doing here? Didn't you want to go to the party?" She then realized Steve was nowhere in sight. Both parents looked at each other and immediately realized what had happened. Never have they laughed so long and so hard (or driven so fast, to make the switch).

AGE 4 to 6
TRICKS OF THE TRADE

Twin Rivalry, Sibling Rivalry—The Attention Game

Ever feel like there are days when you just can't win? And all you wish for is another one of *you*? Get used to it. There's no getting around the fact that there's only one of you and at least *two* of them. You will always be outnumbered. While every family dynamic with twins is different, one thing remains the same: your twins have had to share and compete for your attention since birth, and that's never going to change. As with most competitions, rivalry is likely to ensue. Plus, if there's another sibling or two involved, you may as well just shoot yourself now (just kidding). At times, it seems like someone in your house is always upset with you. This is what you hear: "You gave him more than you gave *me*" or "Why was *her* story longer than mine?" or my favorite, "It's not fair!" I hate to be the bearer of bad news, but it doesn't seem to get better with age. Sorry. On top of vying for your attention, your twins are also working out the dynamics within their own relationship. Add in a sibling, and the mix can get quite complicated, to say the least. That said, there are many ways to help foster a sense of uniqueness and individuality among your twins and their siblings, thus lessening the rivalry between them. All it takes is a little ingenuity and time (and perhaps a scientific breakthrough in the cloning process of adult females).

Twin competition

Every child wants to be seen as an individual, with an identity separate from her siblings. This is especially true with twins. While the twin bond can often be all-encompassing, twins trying to establish their own individuality are influenced by many factors, two of the most influential of which are you and your partner's attitudes about the twinship and what the twinship means to the twins themselves. If parents view their twins as a unit who are supposed to do *everything* the same, then their twins are more likely to view themselves this way, too. If, on the other hand, you and your partner have always treated them as separate and unique, your twins are more likely to view themselves this way. Being treated as individuals enhances their ability to maximize their different strengths while still embracing their twin bond. Some parents fall into the trap of labeling their twins early on to accentuate their differences. You may hear parents calling one of their twins the "good" twin, the "social" twin, the "shy" twin, or the "assertive" twin, just to name a few. Try not to do this. You'd be surprised how often kids try to live up to this label, even if it's negative. Truth be told, the balance within your twins' relationship often shifts back and forth. While one twin may be very assertive in public, the other twin may be very assertive in private. Or, one twin may be particularly shy as a toddler, only to outgrow his shyness by kindergarten. Labeling a child only puts undue expectations on her. The key is to *respond* to your children's differences, not *create* them. It's not up to you to give your twins separate identities. They were born that way. But it is up to you to help foster those identities in a positive way. Do realize that twin and/or sibling rivalry is part of everyday life—no matter what you do or don't do. Just because they're twins doesn't mean they should be treated the same. *Fairly*, yes, but not necessarily the same. Different children require different amounts of attention, affection, and discipline. It's up to you as a parent to read between the lines and figure out who needs what and when. When you acknowledge those differences without making comparisons, your twins are more likely to embrace their individuality and respond more positively to being treated differently.

The reality is, no matter how fairly you treat your children, you can't possibly eliminate all rivalry. Which brings us to another charming aspect of four- and five-year-old twins: *fighting.* There's nothing in this world that gets me going as much as when my twins fight. I can feel my blood pressure rising just thinking about it. But, as most child experts will agree, fighting is a normal part of growing up—especially with twins. Fighting between twins often helps them establish independence and individuality. It also helps develop the differences between them. By defining who they aren't, they're clarifying who they are; not only to each other but to the world around them. Some experts agree that fighting may actually make twins closer (although I'm not sure I buy that one). Fighting also helps your kids learn to negotiate, mediate, and problem-solve. These are wonderful qualities to learn as a child and will help them to get along in the world as adults. In fact, a study of adult twins found that those who considered themselves to be healthy, well-adjusted adults believed the competition they felt with their twin growing up had ultimately helped them to develop successful careers and family relationships.

For you, one of the biggest issues that arises from all this fighting is figuring out when to intervene, when to arbitrate, and when to do nothing. While that decision will become a personal judgment call, often your actions (or lack thereof) will be determined by their age, as well as the rules in your household. The younger your twins are, the less able they are to share, compromise, and cooperate. Here's when your refereeing skills will come in handy. As your twins begin to mature, you may be able to step back a bit and let them work it out themselves. They may not care as much now about everything being even-steven; they may care more about getting what they want, i.e., the brownie instead of the cake, or watching one show instead of another. But no matter how old your twins are, some rules should be universal: no hitting, no kicking, no spitting, no throwing objects, and no foul language. If you witness any of the above, that's your cue to intervene immediately. As you probably already know, the intensity of the fighting can escalate rather quickly. Be sure to step in as soon as possible to avoid a full-blown blowout in your house.

When your twins are fighting to get attention from you, it's usually not a good idea to intervene. Not only does your intervening show them that negative attention is better than *no* attention, it interferes with your twins' ability to learn how to resolve their own conflicts. There will be many days when it feels as though your twins are following you around measuring everything you do for one against what you did for the other. Relax—this is normal. While this type of behavior may be utterly annoying to you, complaining about favoritism is a rite of passage for twins.

Here's how you can help ease the rivalry:

1. **Spend time alone with each twin.** This doesn't mean your time together must be spent doing some grandiose activity. Get an ice cream cone, take a stroll

around the block, even sit in the yard together. I've done this with my twins ever since they were babies. Not only does it allow each of them to have their own special time with you, *you* also benefit by being able to focus on just one child. Whenever I spent time alone with one twin, I witnessed a whole new side of him or her. Because they didn't have to compete for my attention, each child was much more relaxed and able to be themselves. I was constantly surprised and delighted to learn about their thoughts on life *and* their twinship. It's really a wonderful way to get to know your child as an individual instead of a twin. Plus, their "twin radar," which is constantly turned on looking for *any* inequities, suddenly turns off. And that alone makes it worthwhile.

2. **If possible, get grandparents involved.** As my own mom often reminds me, "Being a grandparent is better than being a parent. You get all the joys without any of the responsibilities." If you are fortunate enough to have grandparents living nearby, try to make them an integral part of your twins' lives. Many grandparents shower unconditional love on their grandchildren. And that extra attention may be just what your twins need—not to mention giving you a break at the same time.

3. **Do not show favoritism.** This will only increase hostility between your twins. If one twin feels the other

twin is the "preferred" child, he or she will most likely feel the need to not only fight harder with the twin, but to fight harder with *you* for your attention, as well.

4. **Try not to make comparisons.** Comparisons only serve to promote competitiveness. Instead of comparing behavior or talents, highlight things each twin is good at. For example, if one twin is unable to set the table correctly, but is able to fold the napkins, acknowledge her napkin-folding ability as a job well done. *Do not* make the mistake of saying, "Why can't you learn to set the table like your sister?" That will only serve to instill a sense of competitiveness and jealousy in your twins. Also, make sure to show appreciation for each child's individual talents. If one twin is an excellent painter while the other is a talented soccer player, make sure to point out and acknowledge each child's strengths.

5. **Let them know things can't always be equal.** Equitable, yes—but that doesn't always mean the same. No two children are exactly alike; therefore they shouldn't be treated exactly alike. As I stated earlier, if you can acknowledge the differences between your twins without making comparisons, they will be more likely to accept and value those differences. That makes it easier for each child to appreciate their own individuality as well as accept being treated somewhat differently than their twin.

6. **Let each child know they are special for reasons other than being a twin.** Let's face it, most people are fascinated by twins. And twins are often given special attention from just about everybody in their lives because of it. Make sure that being a twin doesn't become your child's entire identity. Praise their individuality and let them know how much you love them for who they are, both as part of a pair *and* as an individual.

7. **Give them plenty of time apart.** Each child needs time to be alone—alone with you and alone with friends. Not only will this help them appreciate the time they *do* spend together, it will lessen the rivalry and competitiveness between them.

8. **Encourage independent decision making.** Just because your twins are part of a unit doesn't mean they have to like and do everything the same. Let them know it's OK to be different and to like different things or different people. Encourage them to think for themselves and to make decisions based on their own likes and dislikes. But do let them know that thinking differently doesn't take anything away from their twinship. Remind them that their twin bond will be with them for the rest of their lives.

Sibling competition with the twins

Whether you have an older sibling to multiples, a younger sibling to multiples, or both, one thing is for certain: all children like to be valued for who they are as individuals, not for who they are in relation to someone else. In most families with twins, the twins usually end up taking center stage, thus leaving a sibling to try to figure out just where he or she fits in. The good news is that most siblings of twins take it upon themselves to find a way to fit into the group and are usually successful in finding a place for themselves. In most cases, the sibling just wants to be extra sure that indeed there *is* a place for him or her in the family. But it's up to you as a parent to make sure the "singleton" sibling is not continually eclipsed by the twins.

Siblings of twins can often have a difficult role. The older sibling of multiples may feel as if he or she is being dethroned upon their arrival. The younger sibling of twins may find it hard to catch up to them and difficult to compete with them. Despite the difficulties, most parents agree that all of their children eventually develop individual relationships with one another despite the twin factor. Don't forget, these relationships are very fluid. It's not uncommon to watch the dynamics between your children change from day to day—sometimes from moment to moment. From archenemies to best friends and then back again: it's all in a day's work for some families. On the other hand, if you find your singleton child is having a hard time adjusting to his twin sibs, he may react in one of the following ways:

1. He may try to "become" one of the twins by emphasizing how much he is like his siblings.

2. He may try to separate the twins to minimize the closeness of the multiple relationship.

3. He may try to get one twin on his side and exclude the other.

If this is the case in your household, encourage opportunities for the sibling to spend one-on-one time with each twin. Also, try to make sure you and your partner are setting the appropriate twin "tone" in your household. Remember, if you treat your twins as individuals instead of a unit, your other child(ren) will pick up on this, making it less likely that the sibling will feel a rivalry with the twins. Do realize that no matter what you do, there is no way to ever completely eliminate sibling rivalry or the competition for your attention. It's just another fact of life with children. While you can't control it, you *can* help your children deal with it by how *you* choose to handle it.

Real-life rivalries from the twin trenches

Interestingly enough, when I spoke to parents of twins about the family dynamics in their households, I realized there were as many different scenarios and rivalries as there were children involved. While all children obviously competed for their parents' attention, the dynamic between the twins and their siblings was specific to each family. Do any of the following situations sound familiar?

Tami O. has four-year-old fraternal girls and a seven-year-old girl. She says the rivalry in her family is strongest between one of the twins and her older sister. Tami thinks it's because both of these girls have very dominant, independent personalities.

Isabelle R.'s five-year-old identical girls worship the ground their twelve-year-old brother walks on. But the feeling wasn't always mutual. When the twins were younger, their older bother used to look upon them with disdain.

Suzan C. has four-year-old identical girls and a five-and-a-half-year-old boy. She says the rivalry is equal between all three. While they all play very well together, the rivalry usually rotates around a toy that one of them wants.

Jacquelyn P. has nine-year-old identical boys and an eleven-year-old son. Her twins are extremely close and go out of their way *not* to show each other up. They also look up to their older brother like a "king" as he really seems to take care of the twins. Their bond is so tight that if Jacquelyn decides she wants to discipline one of the three, the others try to talk her out of it.

Kimberly S. has two-year-old fraternal girls and a four-year-old daughter. She says the rivalry in her house is stronger between the twins themselves than between the twins and their big sister.

Meghan B. has two sets of twins (and you thought *you* were busy): four-year-old fraternal boys and one-year-old boy/girl twins. One of the four-year-old twins has such an intense rivalry with the one-year-old girl twin that he goes a little crazy whenever he sees her. He screams, rolls around on the floor, lies on top of her, jumps around her high chair, and occasionally throws toys at her. On the other hand, the other four-year-old twin couldn't care less about the two younger twins and focuses his feelings of rivalry on his twin brother. Go figure.

Whether or not you recognize your own family's dynamics in the above scenarios, one thing is for certain: the relationship between the twins themselves and the one they have with their siblings can be calm *or* contentious, or a confusing combination of the two. Good thing the expectations each child has for him- or herself and for others change as the child develops. Best friends one day, worst enemies the next. Don't worry about it, but do expect it. That's life with twins.

How's Your Marriage Holding Up?

Let's talk statistics. According to the National Center for Health Statistics, data from 2003 shows the marriage rate to be 7.5 per 1,000 total population and the divorce rate to be 3.8 per 1,000 total population. Guess what? That makes the divorce rate to be right about 50 percent, or 50.6 percent, to be exact. As if that number isn't high enough, consider this: it's even *higher* in families with multiples. Some studies indicate that higher stress levels among families raising twins and higher-order multiples have led to a divorce rate *two* to *three* times higher than the divorce rate in the general population. Yikes. While you'll read more about how divorce affects kids in Age Six to Ten Reality Check, let's focus on something much more positive (hopefully): your marriage.

To be honest, some may think I'm not the best person to be spewing advice about marriage. Truth be told, I became a statistic. My husband and I divorced when my twins were very young. And while it would be easy to say my marriage woes were the result of having multiples, that just wasn't the case. As with most marriages, the problems were present well before the arrival of twins. The stress of multiples just seemed to exacerbate our problems. That's the good news. The bad news is how easy it is to let your marriage fall through the cracks because of a shift in focus. Well, a really *big* shift in focus. Mix that with the added financial strain of twins, sleepless nights, and perhaps a two-career household, and even the healthiest of relationships can begin to fracture. In a 1992 National Organization of Mothers of Twins Clubs survey on divorce, 39 percent of the respondents felt that the added emotional stress of having multiples contributed to the breakup of their marriages. And a whopping 75 percent found their marriages beginning to deteriorate within the first three years of their multiples' lives. No one said juggling marriage and twins would be easy. But many learn how to make it work—and make it work well. Let's talk about the importance of staying connected and how to consistently make time for each other so neither of you will ever have to worry about becoming a statistic.

Be aware of potential causes of conflict

Breakdown in communication. Most therapists will agree that one of the biggest causes of conflict in a relationship is lack of communication. Sometimes this happens simply because you don't spend enough time spent together. Or because you're exhausted. For others, it may stem from a buildup of resentment over parenting duties or household chores. And then there's the denial thing. If you don't talk about a problem, then maybe it's not really happening or will go away on its own, right? Having twins also creates complex parenting issues that parents of singletons just don't have to deal with. Such as: How will you dress your twins? How will you discipline them? Will they share their toys or get their own? Who's on diaper duty when? If you're like most parents of multiples, you probably never thought about these questions, let alone discussed them, prior to having twins. Or if you did, you just assumed you and your spouse would be on the same page about everything. Remember what you learned in Communication 101? Don't ever assume. "It makes an ass out of . . ." well, you probably know the rest. Anyway, if you find you and your spouse drawing lines in the sand over some of these issues, don't despair. Just because you didn't anticipate feeling differently about these issues doesn't mean you can't work through them. Communication can be hard work. Sometimes it takes time and effort, not to mention a cool head, to come to terms. On the flip side, lack of communication can have dire consequences for any relationship.

Power change in the relationship. If your relationship is like many others, the person who spends the most time with the twins ends up being the one who establishes their routines. This can include playtime, naptime, eating, and bedtime schedules. That can cause the other parent to feel a loss of power in the relationship—not to mention feeling left out. If this is happening in your relationship, make sure the one who is establishing the rules discusses them with the other parent *before* they're implemented. This way, both parents have a say and become partners in the parenting decisions being made. This will help to eliminate any ongoing power struggles or feelings of being marginalized as a parent.

Lack of time for each other. Talk to any parent with young kids and you'll hear the same thing: "We never have time for each other anymore." If you want to stay married, I suggest you make that time together a priority. Read on for tips on how to create that time and how to focus on your relationship again.

Different parenting styles. No two people can agree on everything. And that includes how to parent. The reality is that you had different upbringings and different experiences that you bring to the table. It's OK to have different philosophies, just as long as you can come to a meeting of the minds about key issues such as discipline, money, and time spent with the kids. Consistency is key. It's very confusing when one parents says or does things one way and then the other parent contradicts those things. Kids are smart and can pick up on dissension pretty quickly. Obviously, this can rock their stability. Make sure you're able to talk things through with each other and find some common ground. While you can't expect to agree on everything, you should at least try to support each other whenever possible—at least in front of the kids.

How to make time for your spouse

Children do best in happy homes, period. And if you choose to make that happy home with two loving adults, then your relationship should stay at the top of your priority list. The best thing you can do for your children is to maintain a happy and loving relationship with your spouse. Not sure how to go about "keeping the love alive" now that your family has doubled in size? Here are a few tips to consider:

1. **Find a way to connect during the day.** Whether it's a quick "I love you" on the phone or, better yet, a plan to meet for coffee or lunch, make sure to reach out to

each other every day. Flowers for no reason? A sure bet. Breakfast in bed? Even better. A surprise weekend getaway? A home run. Remember, often it's the little things we do that can make a difference in how we feel about our spouse and how our spouse feels about us.

2. **Plan a date night.** If you can, try to plan a night once a week for just the two of you. Planning an evening out with your spouse involves lots of anticipation, and that alone can get you to refocus your attention on your relationship and feel excited again. If hiring a babysitter makes weekly date nights too costly, find other resources. Grandparents, aunts and uncles—even the teenager down the street may be more than willing to pitch in. Or, try to join in a babysitting co-op with other parents. You may not get to go out quite as often, but at least you'll be able to plan ahead and look forward to your upcoming "date night."

3. **Reclaim your own bed.** For many years, I was sure I was married to twin toddlers. Each morning I'd wake up to find two beautiful sleeping babies next to me. My husband was out on the couch (and you wonder why I got a divorce?). I'm sure many of you can relate. It's not uncommon for a toddler or two to sneak into their parents' bed, making it impossible to be alone together. No matter how you choose to do it, try to reclaim your bed.

Today. Maybe you can start by making three nights a week a "no-kid" zone in your bed. Not only will this help to kick-start your relationship, you may even be able to catch up on your sleep.

4. **Schedule time alone with your spouse.** If getting out of the house with your spouse is just too difficult, try at least to schedule some time alone. Whether it's when the twins are napping, after they have gone to sleep in the evenings, or when they're busy playing with each other, spend some time focusing only on each other. And make sure to have a "no cancellation" policy. It's pretty easy to blow off your scheduled time together when you have piles of laundry to do, a stack of bills to be paid, or missed sleep to catch up on. Try not to. Remember, finding time to be together should be a top priority. You've always got tomorrow to deal with all the really boring stuff you didn't get to today.

5. **Go away for a weekend.** Or even for just one night. And make sure to plan something romantic. It's not often you'll have an *entire* night or two to yourselves, so make sure to take full advantage (wink, wink). I think you'll be amazed at how quickly you can reconnect with your spouse when you don't have to split your attention among three or more people. I often found that one of the best things about going away was

coming home: not only did I feel relaxed and refreshed, I couldn't wait to see my twins after being away.

It's OK to get professional help

There are times when, no matter what you do or try, you can't seem to get your relationship back to the way it was. Don't feel alone. Many couples reach this point and don't know where to turn. This may be the time to seek professional help. For those of you who feel there is a social stigma attached to seeing a therapist or who may be too embarrassed to ask for help, don't be. I know of many couples that have gone to marriage counseling at different points in their relationship, with great results. Whether you feel it's best to seek help on your own or as a couple, asking for help is one of the bravest things you can do. Besides, if the end result is a happier, more fulfilling relationship for you and your spouse, you have absolutely nothing to lose. On the flip side, getting professional help may help you come to the realization that you are better off ending the relationship than staying in it. Sad as that may be, at least you're actually doing something about it instead of remaining stagnant in a potentially toxic situation. Remember, doing what's best for you now is what's best for your children in the long run. When one door closes, another usually opens.

Note to single parents

Yes, raising twins alone can be a daunting task. And yes, you may be faced with additional financial and emotional stresses.

But hey, as you've already discovered, marriage isn't all it's cracked up to be. There can be some surprising benefits to single parenting. Consider the following:

- You, and only you, get to make the rules.
- There will be no more fighting with your spouse (at least not in the same house!).
- There will be less tension in your home.
- You get to make all the decisions, like what time your twins go to bed, how to dress them, and how to discipline them.
- Who cares if they sleep in your bed?
- And best of all, your twins don't care if you're married or single. They'll love you the same no matter what your marital status is.

At the end of the day, try to keep your sense of humor. Realize you don't have to be perfect. Make sure you're getting the support *you* need and your kids will do just fine. Do the best job you can, and know that that's good enough.

Going Back to Work . . . or Not

Most of us remember this familiar scenario: you finally get the news—you're pregnant. You're ecstatic. You and your partner have been planning financially and emotionally for this moment for quite some time. You've even worked out the perfect scenario for your family once the baby's born: you've decided to quit your job and stay at home while your partner continues to work. Then you get the news. Not only are you pregnant, you're pregnant with *twins*. In an instant, your entire life changes. Then reality sets in. All of a sudden, your plans seem to go *poof.* New questions arise: How does this affect you financially? Will you have to return to work? What about child care? Can you afford child care? How do you take care of two babies at once? The list goes on. Boy, I remember going through this like it was yesterday. I was an account executive for a radio station in Los Angeles. I had been with the station for eight years and was at the top of my game. I had worked long and hard to gain my status and wasn't going to let a baby or two get in the way. Like I said . . . the best-laid plans. I had fully intended to return to work after my maternity leave of just eight weeks—until I realized after the eight weeks were over that I had yet to get more than two hours of consecutive sleep in that whole time. Not to mention the big dark circles under my eyes, spit-up on my clothes (the ones that still actually fit me), and a brand-new nonprofessional way of thinking. More importantly, though, something else happened to me. In the midst of all those feedings, changings, and burpings, my priorities shifted.

Taking care of my newborn infants and being there to see those first two smiles versus schmoozing with the next big client over lengthy, boring dinners and sporting events? It was a no-brainer.

While this may be a familiar story to many of you, the reality is that making work-related decisions affects not only you but your entire family. Plus, that decision often involves a bevy of emotions. It can bring up issues of self-worth, guilt, accountability, and trust, just to name a few. To top it off, there's no right or wrong decision. For many, it's not even a choice. They simply have to return to work for financial reasons. For others, the decision involves compromise: what if you want to go back to work but your partner wants you to stay home? Or vice versa? The only right decision is the one that's right for you, and for your family. That's it—there's no magic to it. So, whether you tinkered with the idea of going back to work after your twins were born and never quite made it, or you went back and are now wondering what it might be like to be a stay-at-home mom, you're not alone. Just make sure your decision comes from the heart. A fulfilled and happy parent usually means a happier home life overall.

Just the stats

If you're wondering just how many moms are currently in the workforce, wonder no more. According to the United States Department of Labor, Bureau of Labor Statistics, working moms account for almost one-fifth of all employed individuals and nearly three-fourths of them work full-time. Currently, seven out of ten mothers are in the labor force, compared with just five out of ten in 1975. And these moms are busy. The mothers who work full-time are also spending more than two hours each weekday taking care of their children, cooking, and cleaning house. Plus, nearly four out of ten moms who work full-time also do volunteer work at some point throughout the year. Talk about a hectic lifestyle (which I'm sure most of us can relate to).

Finding balance

Some people thrive on being a stay-at-home parent. Others feel working full-time is what's best for them. I prefer to balance the two. Working part-time is what works best for me—I truly feel it makes me a better parent. But that's me. Everyone must find her own sense of balance. Sometimes you have to be very creative to find it. Consider the following scenarios:

Scenario 1: You've been working full-time for what seems like most of your life and would like to see if you can modify your situation to be able to spend more time with your family. Here are a few things you need to consider:

1. ***Health insurance***—If you're thinking about quitting your job and are currently receiving health insurance benefits from your employer, you must think ahead. Gone are the carefree days of quit now and worry later.

If you leave or lose your job, you are eligible for COBRA insurance for an additional eighteen months (sometimes longer, depending on the circumstances). But unfortunately, you have to pay the insurance premiums yourself. If you're married, another option would be to get coverage from your spouse's policy. Just make sure you find out what your insurance policy covers, as the rules can vary from state to state.

2. ***Financial security***—The reality of your situation may be that you just can't afford to quit your job right now. Let's face it: the cost of raising one child is high enough, never mind raising twins. But if you feel you'd make a better parent by changing your situation, dig a little deeper. If you're married and your spouse is working, try redoing your budget to see if you can live on one income. You'd be surprised at how much you can save by reassessing your needs and making cutbacks. Another solution may be to take a temporary leave of absence from your job. Most employers realize the value of good, loyal employees these days and are usually willing to work with them to accommodate their needs.

3. ***Personal identity***—If your self-worth is tied up in what you do for a living, you're in for a double whammy if you quit your job. Not only will you feel the financial loss, you'll be reeling from a full-blown identity crisis.

Of course, there are other ways to define your self-worth besides work. Consider this an opportunity to explore other areas of your life that can provide a similar sense of self-worth. I have a hunch you may not have to look much further than those two smiling faces right in front of you. It's amazing how quickly you will become known as "Billie's mom" or "Emily's dad," even "the twins' parents." Somehow that comes to seem a whole lot more important than winning that trial or making that sale. Believe me, being a parent is probably the single most important and fulfilling job you'll ever have.

4. ***Quest to be superwoman***—The debate of whether women can have it all and do it all rages on. But a new question also comes into play: do you really *want* it all? In my opinion, the quest to be superwoman is highly overrated. Who needs that kind of pressure? Sure, if running a corporation is what's best for you, great. Just as long as you're doing it for *you* and not because you feel like you have something to prove. Balancing career and family is a constant juggling act. Many women feel as if they can't give their all to either. They feel as if they are constantly disappointing someone, be it their family or their boss. Add to that the feeling of guilt, and it's no surprise many working moms are so stressed out. On the other hand, many working moms also feel incredibly

fulfilled both personally and professionally and wouldn't trade the mix for anything in the world—not to mention the positive role model they're providing for their children. But only you can make that decision. And sometimes you have to be very malleable to find just the right balancing act to suit your needs.

Scenario 2: You left the workplace when your twins were born and would like to go back, but don't think you want to go back full-time. What are your options?

1. ***Consider working part-time or flex-time***—If you can find the right fit, this solution can provide you with the best of both worlds. After my twins were born I was lucky to find a flex-time position that allowed me to create my own schedule. Different from part-time, flex-time usually allows you to work the same amount of hours, but you aren't committed to any set schedule. It's up to you to decide which hours and days you need to work in order to get the job done. While flex-timers obviously need to be self-disciplined, the freedom they gain is well worth it. Flex-time was ideal for my situation. It allowed me to get my job done while my kids were in preschool and then have the remainder of the day to spend with them. Part-time, on the other hand, may require you to make a commitment to a set amount of hours or a certain amount of days per week. That may

actually be a plus for some people. The stability of knowing what their week is going to be like ahead of time can offer more consistency and comfort. The good news is, both types of schedules have given many women the opportunity to reenter the work force while still allowing them to have the time they need with their kids.

2. ***Try working from home***—These days, all you need is a computer and a phone to get your job done from just about anywhere. And many employers seem to be very open to the idea of letting their employees work from home two to three days a week. Or, maybe it's time to think about starting your own business. Many moms have been successful at turning a favorite hobby into a full-blown home business. One word of caution: if your twins are home while you're working, you may not get anything done. One way to get around this is to try to get most of your work done while they're in day care or preschool. Or, you may want to hire a babysitter to watch them while they're at home so you can actually get your work done.

3. ***Consider job-sharing***—This is an ideal solution in theory but can be a bit tricky to implement. Not only do you have to find a compatible partner to work with, you also have to make sure the whole process is not

more trouble than it's worth. Although you're supposed to be working less, some overachievers try to cram a full week's work into their shortened week, knowing they have less time to get it done. On the flip side, I know many people who have achieved ideal job-sharing situations and would never consider going back full-time.

In the end, try to keep your perspective. Jobs come and go, but your twins are only young once. In your quest to find the perfect solution, remember: your kids should always come first.

"Nine-to-five" issues you need to ponder

As with everything in life, there is no such thing as a free lunch. You must consider all aspects of your decision when deciding whether or not to go back to work. A few things to think about:

- Make sure to discuss your needs and wants about working with your partner *before* you make a decision. While you may have a certain scenario in mind, your partner probably does, too. Make sure you're both on the same page about it so neither of you has residual resentment about the decision that's ultimately made.

- What's right for one family may not be right for yours. This is not the time to keep up with the Joneses. Just because their life works a certain way doesn't mean yours will.

- Even the best-laid plans change. What was right for you and your family when your twins were born may not be right for you now. It's OK to change your plans as you go along. And it's OK to admit that you made a mistake or have changed your mind.

- Try to always put your kids first. If you have a special-needs child, working full-time may not be the best thing for your family right now. Your child needs you more than your job does. Try not to lose sight of your priorities.

- Don't feel guilty about the decision you've made. There's no need to complicate your feelings with a wasted emotion. Whether it's staying at home or going back to work, you're doing what you think is best, period.

- There is no right answer to the question of which year in a child's life is the most important for you to be there for. They're *all* important. When I was debating whether I should return to work right after my twins were born or whether I should wait another year, I heard it all. There were those who claimed the first year was the best time to go back to work because all the babies do during the first year is eat, sleep, and poop. On the other hand, others were saying just the opposite: the first year is the critical year to stay at home to bond with your children. Again, there's no right or wrong answer; do what's best for you.

- It's OK to be a stay-at-home dad as long as you don't have any notion that your new "job" will be any easier than your old one. In fact, most would agree, it's probably the hardest job you'll ever have. Any thoughts of putting your feet up and watching the game during the day need to go right out the window. Most stay-at-home parents with twin toddlers barely have time to go to the bathroom, let alone relax in front of the TV. Make sure you know what you're getting yourself into before you decide to entirely change your life. Kudos for trying it, though.

- Get a good support system. Whether it's extended family, a babysitter, neighbors, or other twin parents, you must have your resources in place before you go back to work. You and your partner should also decide ahead of time how you want to handle a sick child. Who stays home? Who picks up the child from school? Who takes the twins to doctors' appointments? Not to mention all the unforeseeables: a new project comes up at work, the car won't start, the toilet overflows, the carpool is late, etc. Knowing ahead of time who to call in a pinch will alleviate a lot of the stress when a crisis hits. This is the time when being ultraorganized pays off, big-time.

- Make time for your marriage. If you're both working, make sure the balance of your relationship doesn't shift. It's easy for your spouse to get lost between the new job, the child care, taking care of the house, paying the bills, and everything else. To top it off, most working moms want to spend *all* their time off with their children, making it that much harder for them to make marriage a priority. Be creative. Follow some of the suggestions from *How to make time for your spouse* on page 146: Schedule a lunch together. Hire a sitter once a month. Cook dinner together. Even a catch-up phone call during the day works. Just make sure to make time every day to focus only on each other. Even if it's only a few minutes each day. This is the time when the little things really do count. You'll be happy you did them in the long run. So will your spouse.

- With twins, it's easier to divide and conquer the responsibilities. Unlike parenting singletons, twins often require both parents to pitch in and help. If you've been a stay-at-home parent and are now going back to work, the best solution is to decide up front who's going to do what with whom. And make sure you're not always with the same twin. In the midst of chaos, it's easier to continually take responsibility for the twin you're most comfortable taking care of. Don't fall into this rut. Your twins need to be with both of you. And vice versa.

- Whether your kids are in day care or preschool or at home with a nanny, make sure you feel 100 percent comfortable with their caretaker. Listen to your instincts. If you get a bad vibe from the sitter you just hired or you're feeling unusually anxious about your twins' new preschool teacher, make sure to check things out. Who can focus on a new job when you're constantly worried about the welfare of your children? If you find you need to make a change, do. There's no sense in working if you don't have peace of mind about who's taking care of your children.

- No matter how anxious you are to return to the workplace, expect a period of adjustment—in both your home and professional life. It's easy to freak out when your new situation doesn't go as planned. Be patient and give it time. Soon you'll be amazed at how quickly you have fallen into a routine and then wonder what you were so worried about in the first place.

Be ready for anything

In your quest to reshape your life, make sure to keep an open mind. Opportunities that you may not have considered before may come your way. That can be very exciting. My own professional life has taken quite a circuitous path. I mean, who would have thought I'd be sitting here writing a book on twins! Many parents go through lots of changes in their professional lives once they have kids . . . especially if they have twins. There's no question in my mind that I would have returned to my job at the radio station had I had just one baby. But I didn't, and I've never looked back. On the other hand, many women choose not to leave their careers when they have kids for fear of losing professional status by deciding to take the "mommy track." That's OK, too. In the end, whether you're content just staying put for the time being or deciding to take a new career path, know that certain days will run like clockwork and others will succumb to Murphy's Law. Try to keep your sense of humor and remember: tomorrow's another day.

AGE 6 to 8

Surviving Your Twins' Multiple Moods

Time to take a breather. You've officially survived the terrible twos, potty training, preschool, and kindergarten. Plus, you're probably becoming more familiar with the rhythm of your twins' behavior through various stages of growth. Family outings have become much more tolerable, and life in general seems to have evolved into a somewhat familiar routine. That said, don't get too comfortable. Right about now, you may be wondering what in the world has happened to your adoring five-year-olds. In a nutshell? *You*. Once the center of your twins' universe, you have officially been replaced. But don't get too jealous of your replacement. The new center of their world is themselves.

Evolving identities

It's time to get used to an entirely new dynamic in your life. The duo that clung so tightly to your hands at the start of kindergarten isn't clinging so tightly anymore. Up until now, your twins have viewed themselves in relation to who they are in the family, be it a son, a daughter, a twin, or a sibling. Now, as your children begin spending more and more time with their peers, new identities are formed as a result of these new interactions. They are beginning to relish their newly found independence. They want and need to do more things for themselves. The opinions of their peers become increasingly important, and they become more aware of who notices what. This is often the start of what I call the "anti-affection" stage. Gone are the days of unabashed affection for you. Suddenly, any affection displayed in front of their peers results in an awkward discomfort. Not to worry, though. The momentary sting you feel when this happens has nothing to do with their love for you and everything to do with embarrassment. It's all a normal part of trying to emotionally distance themselves from you. Some kids are more aware of these feelings than others. And like any other developmental stage, some kids experience it later than others. I was able to stretch out the "affectionate period" with my twins until about age ten. I find I can still shower my daughter with physical affection in front of her peers, but my son has begun to shy away from it. However, he's the one who can verbally express his "I love yous" in front of the entire world without giving it a second thought. Every child is different. Try not to take anything personally right now. This emotional distancing is a normal part of their growth and development.

Your expectations of them will begin to change, as well. You'll see a big increase in their communications skills, which means you'll spend more time reasoning with them. As they depend on you less and less to define right and wrong for them, they begin to develop a clearer understanding of the difference between the two. They're also becoming aware that others may have opinions that differ from theirs and that that's OK. Along with this awareness comes the ability to think about how their actions are perceived by others. This is the time when many parents witness a wonderful quality emerging in their children: empathy.

Your job as role model is crucial right now

Never underestimate the influence you have on your children in your everyday lives. Even though your twins may be emotionally distancing themselves from you right now, they're still learning from you each and every day. As your twins begin to function more independently, they still look to you for guidance, support, and supervision. Now's the time to help them hone the skills they'll need to thrive in the outside world. Right now, your children need you more than ever to help them define their emotional reality. Your reactions, attitudes, and judgments help your children to see who they are through your eyes. Make sure to always have realistic expectations; this helps to reinforce their self-worth. Emphasize qualities like being kind, being a good listener, being trustworthy, and being a good friend. Don't forget, children are great imitators. When they see you demonstrating these qualities, they often try to do the same.

Learning about friendship

It's also a good time to talk with your twins about what it's like to be a good friend. They've probably already learned that not everyone they befriend will be like their twin; they may have to change their expectations of other children in order to make friendships work. When problems arise, offer them strategies for solving them and reiterate the qualities needed to be a good friend. Talk about the importance of trust, the ability to share activities and feelings, and the value of being there for a friend when they need you. Eventually they'll draw upon the resources you've provided them and (hopefully) learn the importance of compromise in a relationship. One word of caution: don't be surprised at the revolving rotation of "best friends." Especially with girls. While boys can bond over a game of kickball and are happy playing with anyone who wants to do the same things they do, girls' friendships are much more complicated. They seem to develop more intense relationships than boys and are apt to have fewer companions. Plus, girls are better able to distinguish between acquaintances and close friends, whereas boys' interactions with friends are likely to be within a larger group. If you have twin girls, be aware of the "triangle" effect. With two in a relationship, everything is even-steven. When a third gets involved, watch out. The power dynamic in the trio is constantly changing, and one is bound to be the odd girl out at any given moment. As long as it's not the same girl that's being left out each time, try not to intervene. Children need to learn to be able to work things out on their own. If you jump in every time there's a problem in a friendship, they'll never learn the skills to be able to resolve their own conflicts. Remember, elementary-age kids crave approval from their peers. It is important to teach your children that having everyone like them is not necessary. Having a small circle of trusting, loyal friends is much more important. Other ways you can help your children with their friends include:

- Making sure your children know that their friends are always welcome in your house. The way I look at it, a playdate at your house gives you the upper hand. It allows you to have an insider's view on the interactions happening between your children and their friends. Plus, it eliminates your curiosity about what went on during a playdate at someone else's house. Especially if the friend is one they've never played with before.

- Being friendly and hospitable to your twins' friends. No one wants to feel unwelcome at someone else's house. There have been plenty of times my kids have come home from a playdate and refused to go back because of how they were treated by the parent in charge. By treating your children's friends with respect, it sets an example of how you would like your children to treat your own friends when they are guests in your house.

- Making sure your twins' friends know the rules in your house. Most kids know that every household has different rules. Just because a friend gets to watch cable at his house doesn't mean he can in your house. Make it clear from the beginning what the rules are so there are no surprises or hurt feelings.

- Allowing a little junk food as a snack. As long as it's in moderation, there's no harm in serving a little ice cream or some cookies as an after-school snack (unless, of course, the child is diabetic). Let's face it, good food at a friend's house is an incentive in and of itself.

- Trying your hardest *not* to embarrass your twins in front of their friends. This includes everything from singing along in the car together to using cute nicknames from when they were babies. Yep, we all knew the day was coming when we would become an embarrassment to our kids. Don't take it personally, though; it's just another way for your twins to assert their burgeoning emotional independence from you.

Birthday parties and the whole twin thing

Shared birthday parties seem to be the norm for preschool-age twins but that may begin to change now—especially if you have opposite-sex multiples. While preschool-age children tend to have playmates of both sexes, most begin playing with children of their own sex as they get older. Although a lot of it has to do with classroom placement, typically same-sex multiples develop a core of mutual friends and opposite-sex multiples have separate friends. I certainly found this to be true in our household. But there were exceptions. Many times one twin would invite a friend over only to have the other twin join in on the playdate. While combined birthday parties are certainly easier on you, they may not work so well as your children get older. It all depends on your twins. Some twins don't mind sharing birthdays, gifts, and special days together; others do and take great exception to having just one party to celebrate two birthdays. Because their feelings may change from year to year, talk to your twins a few months before their birthday. If they do want separate parties, this doesn't mean you have to invite the entire class over twice. Be creative. Plan two separate sleepovers on different nights. Or, take one twin with a few friends out to dinner and a movie, then do the same for the other twin another night. Theme parks are always popular, as are arcades.

And you can never go wrong with bowling. You get the idea. Just make sure each twin gets to invite the same number of friends. Even though your twins may not want to celebrate together, they still want everything to be even-steven.

Twins' party etiquette—a survival guide

Twins and parties bring up lots of questions. Keep in mind there are no right or wrong answers. This is all about what feels right to you. Some of the most common questions and concerns include:

1. **What happens when only one twin is invited to a birthday party?** This will become a more common occurrence as your twins get older and is something they will be dealing with their whole lives. Not everything in their lives will be shared. Do acknowledge the sadness and disappointment of the twin who wasn't invited, but at the same time try not to downplay the other twin's excitement about the party. Let him know it's OK to enjoy activities on his own and not to feel guilty about attending. Use this opportunity to do something special on the day of the party with the twin who wasn't invited. Then it becomes a win-win situation for both twins.

2. **Your twins are having a joint birthday party and some of the children invited are friends with just**

one of them. Should you expect a gift for each twin? No, absolutely not. And be sure your twins know this ahead of time to avoid any hurt feelings. Now, if the invitee is friends with *both* twins, then it's not unreasonable for your twins to each expect a gift.

3. **Both of your twins are invited to a singleton birthday party. Does each twin need to bring a gift or can you get away with buying only one gift?** At this age, I do think the birthday girl or boy will feel shortchanged by receiving only one gift from two partygoers. This may not be the case once your twins have reached adolescence. But for now, sending two gifts is the right thing to do. If need be, spend the same amount of money you would have for one gift and find two smaller gifts of lesser value.

4. **Only one of your twins is invited to another set of twins' party and is friends with *both* children. Does your child bring one gift or two?** Absolutely two, no question.

5. **One cake or two?** Always two. Or serve cupcakes.

6. **Should your twins give each other gifts?** I say yes, but again, that's a personal decision to make within your own family.

OK, here's my disclaimer: while not everyone may agree with the above solutions, they are how *I* would handle the situations. You may not and that's OK. But do try to think about each situation from a child's point of view—your own child or another's. You may be surprised at how quickly your opinion can change. You just might end up agreeing with me after all.

Grade-level expectations

Your first grader

First graders are wonderful little creatures. They are interested in just about everything and very excited about learning. Their attention spans are longer now and they're ready to be more self-reliant. Teachers focus on self-control. Developing self-control takes a lot of practice, and teachers typically spend a good deal of time going over what's expected of the children in terms of proper conduct in the classroom. Self-control is crucial in order to be successful in school both academically and socially. Those kids that don't learn to regulate their own behavior often have difficulty in the long run. Allow your child to make her own mistakes and make sure not to rush in and solve all her problems for her. Her budding self-esteem will grow and develop from her *own* accomplishments. And if she senses your faith in her abilities, she will learn to trust her own judgments and continue to stay motivated.

A big milestone for first graders is losing teeth. Especially when it happens at school. Whether you believe in the tooth fairy or not, acknowledge the importance of losing teeth in your children's lives. Take lots of pictures. Some of the cutest photos I have of my twins are of them missing their two front teeth—at different times, of course.

What happens when your child's first-grade environment (or that of any grade, for that matter) is less than ideal? Just remember, life is not perfect. Experiencing a less than perfect situation is not the end of the world. It may even help your child to develop healthy coping skills. The key is to learn when to intervene. If your child has a direct conflict with the teacher or is being bullied, set up a conference with the teacher. It's always best to get both sides of the story. But if your child has vague complaints and you suspect she is just experiencing the normal transition period of entering a new grade, hang back and see how the situation evolves. As your twins get older, you'll become more adept at figuring out when they need your involvement. This is a learning experience for you, too.

Your second grader

The second-grade classroom is less boisterous than the first. Most kids have learned how to behave appropriately at school as they begin to learn what's expected of them. At this age, kids are more self-aware and can at times even seem withdrawn. Quite a contrast from your overly confident first graders. Kids are also more attuned to the world around them, and you may observe childhood fears surfacing. Common fears at this age may involve kidnapping or the death of a parent, to name a few. When my twins were at the height of this fearful stage, we had the bad luck of experiencing 9/11. To this day, my son is still afraid of flying. Which brings me to a very important point: one way to help control those fears is to be very aware of what your children are exposed to on television. I'm not so sure my son would feel this way had he not watched the planes crashing into the towers over and over again. While it was very difficult to monitor at the time and almost impossible to avoid due to the intensity of the situation as well as its newsworthiness, I still wonder about its long-term effects on my son.

In responding to your children's fears, make sure to be sensitive to their needs. Remember, kids at this age are adept at worrying and analyzing; they want to make sure they're safe. As your children begin to seek more logic, try to be comforting *and* honest. Let them know they will always be loved and cared for, no matter what.

Your third grader

By third grade, you'll see a big leap in maturity in your twins. More will be expected of them at school as they begin to tackle more complex assignments. No need to worry if they're up to the task, though. You'll also see a big cognitive leap in their abilities. Thinking becomes more abstract at this age, and children begin to have a better understanding of their own individual strengths and weaknesses.

Friendships during this year take on greater importance, and figuring out where they fit in is all part of the third-grade social whirl. Whether it's finding one best friend or enjoying the company of many, developing friendships takes on a life of its own. This is a big step socially and is even more complex for twins.

Especially if they've never been separated. Reiterate the qualities that make a good friend and reemphasize that not everyone they meet will play like their twin. Children of this age are beginning to realize that classmates have different personalities and that it's OK not to like everyone they know. Prepare yourself for some ups and downs during this year as your kids learn how to navigate through and maintain their friendships. Try to be especially supportive of the transitioning friendship between your twins as they begin to learn how to maintain their *own* friendship while trying to make friends with others.

Get involved in school

I can't emphasize enough the importance of getting involved in your children's school, even if you're a working parent. While it's easy to say "I don't have time," I'll throw a little guilt trip at you: I was a single working parent going through chemotherapy and I was still able to volunteer my time on two school committees (sorry!). My point is, many schools rely on parent volunteers to make the school a better one. This includes both public *and* private schools. Volunteering your time doesn't mean you need to take on the job of running the school fund-raiser or even being a room parent. Also, if you can't be physically present at the school to help, there are plenty of ways to help from home. Whether it's helping out with mailings, participating in a phone tree, or doing miscellaneous paperwork, most schools will appreciate *whatever* time you're willing to give.

More importantly, try to make an effort to spend some time in your twins' classrooms these first few years, even if it's only once every few months (remember, though: you have to split the time between their two classes). Before you know it, this window of opportunity will be over as your children may not be quite so thrilled to see you in their classrooms as they get older. Not only does volunteering in the classroom send the message to your child that her school environment is important to you, it allows you to see firsthand how your child interacts with her teacher and peers. Plus, the thrill they get when they see you in their classroom and the smile you see on their faces makes it all worthwhile. One of the biggest benefits to working in the classroom is that it will give you some ideas as to the types of questions you should be asking your twins to help them open up about school. The standard "How was school today?" will usually always result in a one-word response: "Fine." And you've learned absolutely nothing. After spending time in their classrooms, you'll be able to ask more specific questions tailored to their daily activities and experiences. Other hints on helping your children to open up about school include:

- Asking questions when your kids are ready to answer them, not when *you* need to hear them. Many kids need some space after school to process what they've learned that day. Others feel the need to decompress and take a break from school altogether. If this is the case with your twins, don't push. Let them know you're interested in their day and would love to hear about it whenever they're ready to talk. For some kids, that happens at the dinner table. For others, bedtime feels like the most comfortable time to talk about their day. Once they do start talking, you'll be surprised at the delicious details your children will happily provide for you.

- Making sure to stay in touch with their teachers. Some kids just don't like talking about school, period. If you have a child like this, that's OK. Stay informed by communicating with his teacher on a regular basis. But do let your child know that you are in contact with his teacher. Make sure he knows that it's because you'd like to learn more about his classroom and *not* because of anything he's doing wrong.

These first few years of school are exciting ones. Whether your twins are together in the classroom or not, you'll notice each developing new skills as they learn how to be successful individuals at school. Make sure to let them know you're there for them whenever they need you. This may be their first experience away from their twin and they may need additional hugs and support.

Keeping Up with Your Adventurous Dynamic Duo

While the definition of busy never changes, the way you

experience it does. Before, you were busy with diaper duty, toddlerhood, and preschool. Now you'll be busy with pretty much one thing: *driving.* The amount of time you'll be spending in the car schlepping one twin or the other somewhere is enough to make you wish you had a professional driver. Welcome to the world of extracurricular activities. As a parent of twins, you'd better like the kind of car you drive. It will become your second home for many years to come. Your twins' worlds are expanding and with that comes exploration. That means Brownies, karate, Boy Scouts, soccer, baseball, dance class, art lessons, music lessons, swimming, basketball, and gymnastics, to name a few. And that's not to mention playdates, religious commitments, or any school clubs your twins may be interested in joining along the way. Gone are the days of coming home after school and playing with the neighbors on the street or just hanging out. Today's kids have schedules that would tire out the Energizer bunny. Which brings me to a very important point: while it's wonderful to be able to offer your kids different opportunities to enhance their interests or uncover hidden talents, just make sure you're not overscheduling them. Kids need downtime, period. If they're busy from the moment school ends until bedtime, they're not getting it. Not only do your children need time to do their homework, they need time to do absolutely *nothing.* Overscheduling your twins deprives them of free time to indulge in fantasy play or process what they've learned. More importantly, it deprives them of the joys of just being a kid. Kids need to explore the world at their own pace. They need time to figure out who they are and develop their own unique way of handling problems and managing their time. A national study of 3,500 children released by the University of Michigan found that kids today have half as much free time as they did thirty years ago. Children seem to be affected by the same time crunch as their parents. This leaves them little time to recharge their batteries, which is a necessity for everyone. Some kids need more downtime than others. If one of your twins needs more downtime than the other, it's your job to make sure she gets it. Saying no to certain activities becomes a necessity—even if their twin is involved in it. You must reinforce their priorities. Make sure each twin knows that school, homework, and getting enough rest come first, before any outside activities, no matter what.

The good news is that the activities your twins do choose to partake in outside of school help to foster confidence. New activities also challenge kids to set new goals and prompt them to be proud of their accomplishments. When planning your twins' activities, there are several things you should be thinking about:

1. **Allow their interests to develop naturally.** Whether your twins share interests or not, let each twin find his or her own niche. They may both sign up for the same sport, only to find that one loves it and the other hates it. Or, they may choose different activities, only to find they would rather do one together. The key is not to force one to follow the other or encourage them to do separate activities if they want to be together. While it

may be easier on you to schlep them to one activity instead of two, this is the time to let them explore on their own to find out what they like or what they may be good at. Don't be surprised at how fickle they can be, either.

2. **How competitive are your twins with each other?** If your twins have chosen to do the same activity only to find it has created more friction than fun, you must consider how competitive they are with each other. Especially if one twin is more talented in that particular activity. The less talented twin will constantly compare himself to his more talented twin and that can lead to a negative self-image. Getting involved in outside activities should be a positive, pressure-free experience. Try to suggest other opportunities that can highlight individual talents. It can even be the same sport, but different teams. This will allow each twin to feel good about what they're accomplishing as well as highlight their individuality without constant comparison and competition.

3. **What are your goals vs. your twins' goals?** Extracurricular activities are a way to allow your children to explore and enhance *their* interests and talents. Make sure their involvement in certain activities is what *they* want, not what *you* want. Some parents view their children's hobbies as a way to fulfill their own unrealized hopes and

dreams from childhood. Make sure you're not putting your own desires ahead of your children's when helping them decide what they'd like to get involved in. This is for them, *not* for you. And make sure each twin is doing it for themselves, and not just because their twin is.

4. **Are you willing to fully support each twin in the activities they choose?** Some of the activities your children choose may involve an enormous time commitment. And we're not just talking during the week. Many activities include weekend games, performances, and/or practices. If your lifestyle doesn't allow for the time and commitment the activity warrants, *do not* let your child(ren) get involved with it. If you can't be the driver and can't find another, say no. There's nothing more disappointing for the child than allowing him or her to join a team or club only to find out later that the commitment conflicts with your own schedule. Make sure you, as a parent (or another caretaker), are available to fully support the activities your children choose. This means both emotionally and physically.

5. **Are the activities meeting your child's needs?** Some kids thrive in a team-sports environment, while others may need more individual activities. Taking tennis lessons and playing in a soccer league not only require different skills; each activity provides very different

experiences and lessons. Being on a team affords lifelong lessons in learning how to work with others toward a common goal. Art lessons, on the other hand, provide a child with an opportunity to meet individual goals, not to mention enrich their creativity. Try to keep in mind what each child's needs may be when helping them choose their activities.

6. **What happens when your child begins an activity only to find out he or she doesn't like it?** There are two schools of thought on this one. On the one hand, nobody knows what they're going to like or be good at until they try it. There is a lot to be said for children who are willing to put themselves out there to discover their likes and dislikes. If it's an individual activity such as swimming, art, or music class, it's best to be flexible. On the other hand, if your child is involved in a team sport with others counting on him, you may want to think twice if he says he wants to quit. Try to find out what's behind his displeasure. If he wants to quit because someone is bullying him on the team, then you need to speak to the coach and figure out how to resolve the situation. But if he wants to quit because he's not as good as some of the other players and feels inadequate, there's a life lesson to be learned here about not giving up just because other people are better than you. Not only does it teach them that being good at something requires

hard work and practice, it teaches them not to be a quitter. Being on a team, your child learns what it's like to count on other people, as well as to be counted on. Every situation will be different, and you'll need to uncover the specific issues before a decision can be made. But it's best to make sure your twins know your policy on quitting before they commit themselves to certain activities.

8. **Ask for a twin discount.** By now you should be fairly savvy at requesting a twin discount. Sports, hobbies, and activities are no exception. I found most organizations my twins were involved in were more than willing to work with me on cost, even if it was just a 10 percent discount. You have nothing to lose by asking; the worst they can say is no.

Homework: together or apart?

Whether your twins are in the same class or not, comparisons will be inevitable. This includes everything from test scores and daily lesson plans to teachers and homework assignments. My twins have taken it a step further. Not a school day has gone by in which one twin hasn't tried to one-up the other in some way or another. If one comes home from school and says, "My homework is so easy tonight," I can more or less count on the following response from the other twin: "Well, *I* finished *my* homework in class today." Try not to indulge this type of behavior, if at all possible. Your approval or disapproval of either's actions will only serve to heighten the competition. It's very important to point out to your twins that everybody, yourself included, has individual strengths and weaknesses. There's no contest to see who can finish the quickest or who has the easier homework. The most important thing is that each twin is working to the best of their own ability. It really doesn't matter that one twin scored three points higher on her math test than the other. What matters most is that they're both trying their best. When dealing with homework, some twins work wonderfully well together; others do not. While many parents of twins fantasize about their twins being lifelong study buddies, it's best to leave it up to them to figure out what works best.

Other issues to consider:

- **Are they in the same class?** If so, your twins have a built-in study buddy (if they so choose) for that particular year. Not only that, but if one forgets to bring home their book or study guide for the next day's test, there's no need to call all over town to find a friend who can help.

- **How competitive are they with each other?** If doing homework together only increases the competitiveness between them, make sure to set up separate workstations where they can work on their own.

- **Is one twin more willing to help than the other?** This scenario can play out in two ways: either the twin who is *not* willing to help will learn *how to* from his twin, or, the twin who *is* willing to help may feel angry that the help is not reciprocated. Either way, leave it up to your twins to figure out what works best for them.

- **Will doing homework together cause a fight?** If so, don't force the issue.

- **Do your twins refuse to help or take help from each other?** Sometimes the competition between twins is so fierce, they're unwilling to make themselves vulnerable in front of each other. Some will accept help from anyone else *but* their twin. It's OK to have them work together; just make sure you're available to step in when they *do* need help.

- **Is one twin more easily distracted than the other?** It could be the case that your twins love to work together but only one is able to get her homework done. Make sure the situation is conducive to *both* twins' ability to focus; otherwise, you'll need to separate them.

- **Does one or the other prefer to work privately?** Some kids need to work solo, period. Respect their individual needs and make sure to provide them with privacy if necessary.

Same age, different stage

While you're probably used to the fact that each new age brings marked changes in behavior as well as many new accomplishments, continue to make sure that one twin is not the sole reference point for the other. This is especially true when it comes to intelligence. While identical twins will most likely exhibit similar levels of intelligence from year to year, fraternals tend to be much more varied. Always keep in mind the fact that intelligence comes in all forms. One twin may ace her math test every week while the other is extremely gifted musically. Or, one twin may not have yet reached his full potential in a particular subject at school while the other twin has. Most importantly, keep in mind that traditional IQ tests have limitations. Standard testing measures only certain kinds of intelligence. Try to make sure to recognize and appreciate the different ways your twins can be "smart" without making direct comparisons. You can't alter their genetics, but you certainly can help influence their environment to ensure school success. A few suggestions:

1. Be encouraging and supportive of each child's abilities and interests.

2. Positive reinforcement will help to increase both their

motivation and the amount of energy they put into their schoolwork.

3. Have high expectations but make sure they're tailored to each twin's innate abilities.

4. Get involved in their school and get to know their teachers. This sends the message that school is important to you and that you care about their academic environment and success.

Curious classmates

Even though the rate of twin births has more than doubled in the last twenty years, kids are still fascinated by twins. As you go through these first few years of elementary school, don't be surprised at the amount of attention focused on your children solely due to their twinship. While some kids thrive on all the attention, others tend to shy away—depending on how they feel about the twinship. In fact, many pairs who aren't as comfortable with their twin status play down the fact that they're part of a set. Obviously, identicals have a harder time doing that than fraternals. I remember some years in school when it took my twins' classmates several months to realize Maya and Evan were twins. This suited them just fine. Talk to your kids about others' expectations of them. Do other kids want to be their friends because it's "cool" to be friends with twins or because of who they are as people? Even though it may be hard for your kids to understand right now, explain to them that it's important not to rely on their twin status to make friends. Plus, make sure they know it's OK to have separate friends. You'll find these first few years of school to be an interesting time socially for your twins. You will, no doubt, find an enormous emphasis placed on their twinship. But this won't last forever. By the time they're preteens, the novelty of their twinship will most certainly have faded. And it's true what they say, kids ask the darnedest questions: Why don't you dress alike? Do you share a lunch? You sure don't look alike. Why aren't you in the same classroom? Do you do everything together? Do you do everything the same way? Why is one of you smarter than the other? And my favorite: You can't possibly be twins; you're not the same sex! Role-play with your children to help them answer these questions both correctly and civilly. Some twins may take offense at such questions and feel like they are being attacked. They may reply with nasty comebacks. Explain to your children that other kids are asking these questions out of curiosity, not malice. This is a wonderful opportunity for your twins to learn how to educate others and to teach them about something they know nothing about. Just make sure your kids give out accurate information. This isn't the last time they'll need to answer such questions. In fact, these early years will provide you with great insight on what your twins can expect at school for many years to come.

Don't be surprised at your twins' need for privacy

Many sets of twins have shared a room since birth. But by the time most children are six or seven, they begin to want a little privacy. Don't be surprised if your twins are beginning to spend more time alone, reading or playing. This is normal. Your twins are also becoming more aware of their bodies and the differences between boys and girls. With this awareness comes modesty. Many kids at this age won't even let their parents into the fitting room when they try on clothes. Right now, it's helpful to respect your children's need for privacy as well as their newfound modesty. If you have opposite-sex multiples who share a room, now may be a good time to separate them if you have the space in your home. If not, try to help them create individual spaces within the same room through room dividers and movable furniture. Be creative and listen to your twins' input.

The cuteness factor

The truth of the matter is that these early years of elementary school are really quite adorable. Children of this age are generally happy to go to school and are usually excited about the newness of everything. They are eager to learn and to please and are becoming more self-reliant. For twins, the development of outside friendships is vitally important during this stage. As a parent, try to sit back and enjoy this time. As your twins navigate their way through these years, be open to what's developing and changing in their relationship. Make sure you're as present as possible. This is an awfully cute stage in your twins' lives. You don't want to miss a minute of it.

COMIC RELIEF FROM THE TRENCHES . . .

"The Dirty Dozen"

One of the hardest things to do when you're by yourself with young children is to figure out how to take a shower while keeping your children safe. It's especially troublesome with twin toddlers, and personal hygiene in our house often took a backseat to their safety. Being the ultraefficient supermom that I am (*not*), I learned to become the world's fastest shower-taker in no time. Who knew you could actually get clean in sixty seconds or less?

Most of the time, I was able to just turn on a video and bribe them to stay put until I could at least rinse the shampoo from my hair. But on this particular day, my kids were unusually energized—which often spelled trouble in my house. I decided to risk it anyway, as I had a meeting to get to later in the day. The second I jumped in the shower, I knew I was in trouble. All I could hear was high-pitched squealing and giggling, in stereo, and I knew they were up to something . . . *bad*. Sure enough, I zipped through my shower and got downstairs just in time to see the last of twelve eggs being haphazardly tossed onto the kitchen floor. After my initial tirade subsided, I very calmly asked them why in the world they would throw a dozen eggs on the kitchen floor. What were they thinking? Both kids very innocently looked at me and replied, "Mom, we were only trying to find the chicks!" as if that were the most logical answer in the whole world. All at once, we laughed until we cried. Seven years later, we moved out of that house. Sure enough, as the refrigerator was being hauled away, remnants of the egg disaster were still clearly visible. To this day, it remains one of our fondest memories of toddlerhood.

AGE 9 to 10

Double Your Pleasure, Double Your Fun

You're officially entering a period of comfortable equilibrium with your twins. While most of you are probably saying, "It's about time!" under your breath, make sure to enjoy every minute of it, as we all know each new stage is very short-lived. The good news is that your twins are now at an age when who they are becoming as individuals can really shine through. For instance, Maya has an innate sense of style and creativity. She has an amazing eye for colors, art, and fashion and can make anything look good, quite effortlessly. When she tells me I look good in an outfit, I know I must, 'cause she sure doesn't hold back when I make poor wardrobe choices. On the other hand, Evan's wit and sophisticated sense of humor make him a popular commodity in any social gathering. He seems to "get" things others don't. Many agree that age ten seems to be the "perfect" age. Not only are ten-year-olds extremely obedient, they seem to be quite pleased with the world around them. That includes you. As a parent, relish this moment. Never again will you receive the same type of "red carpet" treatment you'll get at this age. The unquestioning acceptance of parents and the desire to do what is right are the hallmarks of age ten. How nice to be treated to twice the kindness and twice the respect! Don't get me wrong, ten-year-olds are far from perfect. But, at this moment, it seems like most of their good qualities are fairly exaggerated, which makes life quite delightful. Being the cynic that I am, though, I'm often waiting for the other shoe to drop. I guess that's what adolescence is for.

Nine-year-olds, on the other hand, may tend to withdraw a bit. In fact, at times they may seem downright uninterested in you. They might demand that this separateness be respected and insist upon being extremely independent. However, nine-year-olds can also be extremely anxious—bordering on neurotic. They tend to be worriers and take things especially hard at times. Some complain a lot, many to an unwanted task imposed on them. Sometimes these complaints are expressed through physical ailments such as stomachaches, headaches, and the like. My daughter was the queen of the stomachache/headache excuse in response to something she didn't want to do. Much of it was school-related: homework she didn't want to do, a lesson plan she was uninterested in, that sort of thing. While I took the first few ailments seriously, it wasn't long before I was "on" to her shenanigans. Sure enough, when she realized she wasn't getting the attention she wanted from me, the behavior gradually disappeared. When the peaceful age of ten finally arrived, all was well in our little world.

Constant comparing

At this point, most sets of twins have been in separate classes for a few years now. Even so, the constant comparing remains a top priority to them. Whenever I pick my kids up from school, the chatter begins almost immediately. Each twin wants to talk about the happenings of the day, good and bad. If both have good days, the volume level increases significantly as each twin tries to get the news out the fastest and the loudest. But if one has a good day and the other a bad day, watch out. The twin who has had the bad day will try his hardest to downplay whatever good news his twin sibling happens to be sharing. When this happens, try to make sure each child has the opportunity to share things with you privately, whether it's a concern or a success. While it's important to be cognizant of the twin who may be feeling envious, you also want to show your pride at the other twin's accomplishment and let her know it's OK to feel good about it. If one twin feels guilty about not sharing in a particular accomplishment of his twin, that's OK, too. Sometimes a gentle reminder of the importance of "being happy for those you love" is a good first step.

Your fourth grader

Expect a more challenging year academically for your nine-year-olds as your children get closer to the middle school years. There is much more emphasis placed on the ability to analyze and compare, and you can anticipate more long-term projects and reports. Even the pacing is quicker this year. My twins had one book report due every month for the entire year of fourth grade (and no, they didn't read the same books). While it seemed somewhat excessive at the time, it certainly taught my kids some wonderful skills, such as reading comprehension, spelling, and learning to think "outside the box." As your children's workload increases, they'll also need to become more organized. If your twins will let you, try to help them hone their organizational skills; being organized will make all the difference in how they handle their increasing workloads. This is also the year to make sure your twins have mastered the basics, especially reading and math. If your twins need help in either of these areas, make sure they're getting the support they need, whether it's from you or from a tutor. A word of caution: if you choose to be the one to give your children academic support, make absolutely sure you understand the work. While I know that sounds crazy, I have a little confession to make. My expertise in math leveled off right around the time my kids hit the third grade. No joke. My ability to provide any type of insight or support came to a screeching halt during that year. Third-grade math and beyond ain't nothing like what it used to be. Now my kids know if they have a problem with math, they need to call Grandpa—end of story.

Your fifth grader

As the oldest students of their schools, fifth graders clearly enjoy the role of being top dogs. Their budding social lives take on greater importance and your children, at times, may seem more interested in talking to their friends than to you. They desperately want to appear more grown-up than they are and may "cop an attitude" to show their maturity. Don't be fooled into thinking your twins don't want or need your advice anymore. Just don't expect them to come asking for it—especially since they have each other. Academically, each child's strengths and weaknesses become more apparent, not only to each other but to teachers as well. If one twin is especially proficient in math while the other is an excellent writer, make sure to acknowledge their individual strengths. You don't want their competitiveness to come in the middle of their school successes. While their teachers work hard to keep the kids motivated, they also highlight the importance of independence this year. Allow each child to take responsibility for their own schoolwork and homework; knowing they can succeed on their own will boost their confidence and self-reliance.

On the surface, your twins may seem like they rule the world. But don't think for one second they are feeling anxiety-free about the upcoming changes in their lives. Leaving the familiarity of their school and friends is a huge step. Many are worried about how they will adapt to a new environment. The jump from elementary school to middle school is huge. Make sure your twins know you're there for them each step of the way, even when it seems like they couldn't care less.

Your role as a parent is changing

As your twins mature and change, don't be surprised at the evolution of your own relationship with them. Growing pains can be hard in any relationship; this one is no different. Their growing independence from you and from each other will present you with many new situations to deal with, both positive and negative. Your expectations of each other are also changing. No longer does a fight result in a fit of kicking and screaming. And meltdowns have hopefully become a thing of the past. In their place are reasoning skills that enable you, as the parent, to appeal to your children on an entirely new level. Some parents appeal to their child's self-esteem ("You're much too kind to treat animals that way"). Some use humor to teach a lesson. You may even find you have to use different tactics for each twin. What one twin responds to may not work for the other. As you're feeling your way through these changes, keep in mind that your children are learning that other people's feelings are just as important as their own. This leap in maturity will be enormously helpful when reasoning with your twins; they are much more capable now of not only understanding others' expectations of them, but also of trying to live up to those expectations as best they can. As their moral development continues to evolve, your twins will look to you for confirmation and reassurance on decisions they've made on their own. This is quite a milestone. How you react is of the utmost importance. Kids are very sensitive to nonverbal expressions. Make sure your body language and actions mirror your words.

As each twin continues to mature at their own pace, remind yourself that it's OK to have different expectations of them. Especially if you have boy/girl twins. As you know, girls typically mature faster than boys. Make sure your expectations for each are realistic based on their individual levels of emotional maturity.

Under the influence of their peers

As your twins finish their final year of elementary school, you may have begun to notice a shift in their social relationships. Relationships with parents and family begin to take a backseat to relationships with their peers. While some parents may experience a temporary sting from this new dynamic, rest assured that the ability to form close friendships is a critical element of their psychological growth and maturity. The most noticeable shift in these relationships actually takes place in middle school, though it's not uncommon for some of these changes to begin occurring right now. Some of this "shifting" may be quite subtle. One day, out of nowhere, your child begins to place more value on a friend's opinion than on your own. Or, all of a sudden your child has an intense liking for a rock band she's always made fun of in the past. When you question her about it, you find out it's her best friend's favorite band. Never underestimate the influence your twins' peers can have on them. Also, don't be surprised if one of your twins is more "under the influence" than the other. Depending on the dynamic between your twins, as well as the dynamic between you and them, one may be more ready than the other to forge ahead with new relationships. If this is the case with your twins, be prepared for some feelings of jealousy. The twin who isn't quite as ready to forge ahead may feel left out, especially if the relationship has changed from a trio to a pair.

As they see their children's friendships begin to grow and mature, many parents begin to worry about their children getting in with the "wrong crowd." If you find either of your twins gravitating toward questionable kids, encourage relationships with kids whose behavior you feel more comfortable about. Suggest activities they can do together and remind them of the common interests they share. While troublemakers may hold a passing appeal (often due to the allure of greater freedom from parental rules and expectations), most children tend to make healthy choices when it comes to friends—especially if they've grown up in a caring and supportive environment.

That's not to say you won't ever have to deal with cliques, social pressures, and the desire of your twins to "fit in." Your twins are defining who they are and who they aren't in relation to their peers. While most kids tend to choose friends who share their values, interests, and outlooks, the pressure to fit in can be overwhelming. Some kids may *still* want to befriend your children simply due to their twin status, but typically by this age kids become more discerning about whom they choose as friends, and more tangible qualities take on greater importance.

When each twin responds differently to the same situation

Behavior, good or bad, is essentially a form of communication each child uses to express needs and feelings. It is influenced by each child's desires and temperament as well as by your own parenting style. What's considered "normal" behavior is determined in part by the context in which it occurs, as well as each child's level of development. The difference between what's normal and what's abnormal may not always be clear. With twins, you have a direct comparison of behavior that parents of singletons don't. That said, it's not uncommon for your twins to react somewhat differently to exactly the same situation. Each child may be trying to communicate a different message through their behavior. In any one scenario, one twin may be trying to communicate, "I'm tired," while the other twin may be trying to say, "I want you to pay attention to me."

Most children will do whatever it takes to have their needs met. Many will go to great extremes to know that unconditional love is there for them. If positive behavior doesn't get them what they want, it's not uncommon for them to turn to negative behavior, even if it gets them a negative reaction. In their eyes, any recognition is better than none. Children are very quick to learn which types of behavior get their parents to respond to them and meet their needs, and are willing to do just about anything to seek the attention they desire.

The behavior your twins exhibit may be impulsive or planned, positive or negative, predictable or unpredictable. And while there are fewer areas that raise more concern for parents than their children's behavior, there isn't a one-size-fits-all fix.

As your twins try to express thoughts, feelings, and needs, always remember they are two separate people and may be trying to communicate different things. As with everything else you've learned about twins, what works for one may not work for the other. Although it may be hard to keep your perspective when dealing with unwanted behavior, try to keep in mind what your twins need most: to be loved, valued, accepted, and respected. After all, isn't that what we *all* need?

Smooth Sailing, Home Free

If there were ever a time to sit back, relax, and enjoy the show, now is it. Make sure to take full advantage of this peaceful time with your twins and help them to enjoy their final year of elementary school. My twins had a ball in fifth grade. Finally they were the "big kids" on campus and they loved every minute of it. Whenever I was helping out at school during my twins' final year, I was amazed at the amount of positive energy floating around their classrooms. Most of the kids seemed generally happy with themselves and their surroundings. As middle school looms, your children realize they are on the brink of a major transition. Toward the end of the school year, you may notice them feeling more apprehensive than normal. Middle school is a big jump and your kids are starting to internally prepare themselves for the upcoming changes. Reassure your twins that they are not alone and, in fact, are much luckier than their singleton friends right now. Not everyone has a twin to share the ups and downs of new experiences with. Whether or not they choose to rely on each other—well, that's a whole other story. As the saying goes, you can lead a horse to water but you can't make it drink.

As a parent, you too may be feeling the sting of an era ending. I sure did, especially toward the end of the school year. While other parents ease into these transitions one child at a time, you've got a double whammy to deal with. Take that into account on the days when you find yourself feeling unusually teary. On the other hand, if you think your twins are growing up too fast, they probably are. Young kids in today's society have a degree of worldliness that many parents have a hard time adapting to. Keep reminding yourself that your children still need firm rules to live by, as well as consequences for breaking those rules. Setting limits for your preteens should remain a top priority. If you have an older sibling in the house, it's more important then ever to make sure your twins don't have the same privileges he or she does. It lets your twins know that their sibling had to wait to attain more "grown-up" privileges, and so do they.

Sex education

If you haven't spoken to your twins about sex yet, just wait. As your children get closer to adolescence, the whole boy/girl thing takes on a life of its own. Comments like "Who passed a note to Sara in class?" to "Did you know Justin has a crush on Chloe?" will start to become normal dinner conversation most nights. But when the "crush talk" involves one of your own, you may find yourself listening more closely. You may even begin to wonder what having a crush means to kids in today's society. And you should. While your twins are decidedly still innocent children, make no mistake about it: they have been paying close attention to how the world works around them, including sex, love, and relationships. In addition, your twins have been exposed to the media's sensationalistic representations of sex and gender, which can cause an awful lot of confusion about what's real and what's not. In today's world, when it comes to their children's sexual upbringing, many parents are just as confused as their kids. Parents have been afraid of overwhelming their children with "too much, too soon" and instead provide "too little, too late." Eventually, their children come to their own conclusions about what's right and what's wrong, and will simply take what they see or hear at face value, whether it's from the media or from their peers. Professionals recommend that sex education be a gradual but steady and proactive educational process starting when children are very young. It's your job as a parent to become that educator. After all, don't *you* want to be the one to get to your children first to instill in them your own values about sexuality? Or, at the very least, help them get the facts straight? When my twins were six years old, our nine-year-old neighbor took it upon herself to tell my children about the facts of life—quite inaccurately, I might add. Luckily, my children immediately ran home somewhat stunned by what they were just told, and I was able to give them correct information in language they could understand. Obviously, this was *not* the way I would have preferred for them to learn about the birds and the bees. But it did open the door to an age-appropriate discussion about sex that became a springboard to many more successful discussions throughout the years.

The truth of the matter is that there are no hard-and-fast rules about what to say to your children and when. As you know, all children have unique temperaments and develop intellectually, socially, and emotionally at their own pace. You may find one twin is ready for more information than the other. Health educators say that one of the best things you can do for your children is to model an open and inviting attitude toward both the physical and emotional aspects of sex. Also, try to be up-front about both the positives *and* the negatives. Today's savvy kids have been hearing about AIDS, teen pregnancy, and sexual assault through magazines, television, advertisements, and peers for quite some time. As a parent, you would be doing your children a great disservice by trying to protect them from the "bad" things by ignoring them altogether. Try to incorporate these issues into an age-appropriate conversation that makes your twins aware of these issues *without* scaring them. The most consistent finding in sex research over the past twenty-five years confirms that children who grow up in families where sexuality is openly discussed grow up healthier. Sexual knowledge is essential to a responsible life.

Now, getting back to the "crush" thing. When my twins were in fifth grade, many kids thought it was cool to "pair off" and become part of a couple—whatever that meant. It seemed each child's definition of what it meant to be part of a couple was different. As crushes begin to take on a new level of importance in your twins' lives, use it as an opportunity to openly discuss friendship, expectations, respect, trust, intimacy, and, yes, sex. Not only does this allow you to get a peek at where your child is emotionally, you may be pleasantly surprised to hear that a crush at their age is just what you remember it to be: a good, old-fashioned, hands-off, friendly, run-of-the-mill crush. Do make sure your twins don't tease each other about their respective crushes. These are sensitive times. There's nothing worse than sharing private information with someone you think you can trust only to have it thrown back in your face. Stress the importance of mutual respect between your twins.

Internet safety

According to a 2001 U.S. Census Bureau survey, 72 percent of households with children aged six to seventeen had a computer in the house and 64 percent of those households had access to the Internet. If your children aren't currently using a computer at home, you can pretty much count on the fact that they're using one at school. In fact, it's not all that uncommon for kids to know more about computers and the Internet than their parents. That's certainly the case in my own house. I have an incredibly savvy computer techie named Evan living right under my own roof. Not only can he solve the most complicated computer snafu, he can type faster than just about anyone I know. But no matter how computer-literate your kids are, they still need your guidance to help them learn how to use the Internet safely. If you are a one-computer family, the first thing to do is to set up computer-use rules with your twins. Setting time limits on computer and Internet use is crucial. We have more than one computer in our house and my twins *still* fight over who gets to use which one when. As the boss (aka parent) of your household, you can actually choose different types of controls you'd like placed on your computer(s). Most Internet Service Providers (ISPs) offer a range of control features; contact your own provider to find out which they offer and then decide which ones would be best for your family. Here are the types of features you may find available to you and what they do:

- ***Kid-Friendly Browsers***—Browsers that do not display inappropriate words or images.

- ***Filtering and Blocking***—Limits access to certain sites, words, and/or images.

- ***Monitoring Tools***—Alerts adults to online activity without blocking access.

- ***Kid-Oriented Search Engines***—Performs limited searches or screen search results.

- ***Block Outgoing Content***—Prevents kids from revealing personal information online.

In addition to using control features, talk to your twins about what they like to use the computer for: Do they like to play video games? Download music? IM (instant message) their friends? Surf the Internet? If so, what sites do they like to go to? Learning about how your children use the computer is just as important as using control features. It not only allows you to open up a dialogue about Internet safety, it shows your kids you're interested in what they're doing. Establish a list of online safety rules for your twins. It's always best to be proactive where their safety is concerned. You may want to include the following:

- Never give out your personal information. This includes full name, address, telephone number, parents' work or cell number, age, or name of your school.

- Never agree to meet in person someone you met online.

- Do not open e-mails or attachments from unknown senders.

- Never send your picture to someone without your parents' permission.

- Make sure the Web sites you're visiting have been approved of by your parents. Do not visit sites that have not been approved of.

- If a Web site, message, or any other type of information found on the computer makes you feel threatened or uncomfortable, make sure to tell your parents right away.

- Don't ever give out your password, unless it's to a trusted family member.

- Don't ever sign up for something that costs money unless you have your parents' permission.

Another feature mentioned earlier that your kids may be using is IM. It allows many kids to be online at once and chat together. Some parents feel the need to monitor this activity in their home. And some kids may feel that's an invasion of their privacy. Remember, you're the parent; it's OK to set rules you feel are necessary to keep your children safe. Just make sure to loosen up a bit as your child matures and becomes more responsible. Once they know you trust them, they'll be reluctant to break any computer rules you set for fear of having their computer privileges taken away.

Computers and Internet usage offer our children a way of communicating and gathering information that wasn't available to many of us when we were growing up. While it may be intimidating to some, try to embrace its importance in your twins' lives. By teaching them how to use it safely *now,* you'll be helping to eliminate potential risks down the road, including loss of privacy, identity theft, joining the wrong chat room, exposure to explicit Web sites, or being lured into dangerous Internet schemes.

Raising socially conscious kids

Most parents these days want to instill in their children a desire to help others. According to the 2000 Cone/Roper *Raising Charitable Children Survey,* 92 percent of American adults believe that encouraging children to participate in charities helps them grow up to be better adults, and 94 percent feel that parents play a key role in getting children involved. Plus, a whopping 85 percent of Americans believe that parents should begin teaching their children about charities before the teen years. The truth is that charitable kids become charitable adults.

The charitable opportunities your twins may have been exposed to through their elementary school, such as toy drives, food drives, and field trips to environmental agencies or to homeless shelters, have provided your children with a hands-on education in doing good deeds and reaching out to the community. Because of such opportunities, your children have been able to feel the sense of pride and accomplishment that comes from helping others. In addition, most of our kids at one time or another have made a card, gift, or comfort food for a sick friend or a grandparent and have experienced the real joy of giving.

Many children involved in Cub Scouts/Boy Scouts or Brownies/Girl Scouts routinely visit nursing homes, plant trees in parks, and collect food and clothing for needy families. And if your twins are involved in a religious organization, they have been exposed to many philanthropic activities over the years. There are many ways to inspire kids to get involved and give back to the community. Consider the following ideas:

- Be a good role model. If you're involved in a charity, talk to your children about what you do for it. Better yet, take them with you to volunteer.

- Encourage children to donate not only their time but their money, too. Have them save a dollar a month (or whatever amount you both decide upon) out of their allowance and donate it to the charity of their choice.

- Get your children involved in youth organizations that emphasize community service. It's never too early to teach your children about the importance of giving.

- Let your children decide what charities to get involved with and how they'd like to donate their time. It can be something as simple as organizing a bake sale to participating in a 5k walk/run.

- Praise your children for getting involved and talk to them about how it makes them feel. Talk about how helping others gives us feelings of value and satisfaction as well as a chance to give back to our communities.

Allow each twin the opportunity to get involved in something that's meaningful and important to them. That may mean getting involved in the same organization but doing different things, or even choosing different charities altogether. The point is to help your twins become more aware of the importance of reaching out to others and how that helps us to feel more gratitude in our own lives.

Preteens already?

For most parents, there comes a day when they look at their twins in awe and wonder how the time went by so quickly. That day came for me when I realized my children were preteens. Preteens! How did this happen? It almost felt like a wake-up call. Suddenly I realized that more than half of their childhood was over—in what felt like the blink of an eye. I began thinking about all those sayings like "Live each day to the fullest," "Live for today," and "There's no better time than the present." They soon became my new mantras. Almost all the parents of twins I know have lived their lives in survivor mode. Often too tired and too busy to actually enjoy their lives, they plod along from day to day until they too experience some type of wake-up call that makes them realize their twins won't be young forever.

Take advantage of this time with your twins before they enter full-blown adolescence. Take the time to get to know them as individuals. Embrace their interests and spend time alone with each child. Take bike rides. Go for a hike. Do silly things that make you all giggle. Bake holiday treats with them. Go to a concert. Go to an art exhibit. Because before too long, your relationship with them will begin to take a major backseat to the ones they have with their peers. Your twins are at an awesome age. Never again will you receive such unconditional love and acceptance. Make the most of this time and expect the best. You won't be disappointed.

COMIC RELIEF FROM THE TRENCHES . . .

"Am I Losing My Mind?"

Jacquelyn P. has identical twin boys named John and Louis. One summer, John developed appendicitis and Jacquelyn rushed him to the emergency room, where they immediately put an IV in his arm. A little while later the other twin, Louis, arrived at the hospital with his dad. Louis decided to go to the bathroom, which happened to be right by the nurse's station. As Louis walked by, the nurse did a double take. How could it be? She was sure he was lying in a bed next door with an IV in his arm. The nurse got a guard to help her bring the "escapee" back to bed. She immediately looked at his arm to see where he'd pulled the IV out and was stunned not to find a *single* mark on his arm. Confusion reigned until Jacquelyn walked in on all of the commotion and explained that the second child was Louis, John's identical twin brother. "Thank God," the nurse said. "I thought I was losing my mind!"

AGE 6 to 10
REALITY CHECK

Dealing with Divorce, Special Needs, and Other Crises

I hate to be a downer, but bad things happen. Marriages fail. People get sick, they have accidents, and so on. As a parent of twins, you may be faced with more than your fair share of issues due to additional risk factors associated with twins, such as prematurity, that parents of singletons just don't have to deal with. While the majority of preterm infants are born without major complications, some parents of twins may find their world shattered by the birth of a disabled twin. Even with all the advances that have been made in today's medical technology, multiple births still involve a higher rate of physical and developmental disabilities than single births.

None of us are immune to crises. We may not always understand why they happen, but we must find a way to deal with them when they do. One of the most important things to realize is that when a crisis does hit, it's not happening only to you—it's happening to your whole family. Don't ever underestimate the importance of attending to the needs and feelings of those around you, especially your children.

The big "D"—how divorce can affect your kids

Let's not beat around the bush. Divorce can be daunting and tumultuous, not to mention downright depressing. And no matter what caused it, it's hard to escape the feelings of loss and heartache. Add in the feelings of guilt for breaking up the family, and your emotions can get the better of you. But wait, who has time to be an emotional basket case when you have children to tend to? Children, who are most likely dealing with many of the same confusing emotions you are, are often left wondering if the divorce is *their* fault. Talk about a train wreck in progress. While you must make time to deal with your own emotions, be it through a therapist, a trusted friend, or a family member, you must also try to make your children a top priority. As hard as it may be, this is the time to refocus your emotional energy into helping your kids deal with their new reality.

Much of what society has learned about divorce indicates that parents can contribute greatly to their children's adjustment. Here are some of the most important things you can do for your children to help reduce the negative effects of divorce:

- Minimize as best you can the conflict and hostility between you and your ex. Above all, try to refrain from speaking negatively about each other to the children.

- Make sure you and your ex are on the same page when it comes to child rearing and discipline issues. Try to support each other's parenting role as best you can.

- Provide lots of structure and routines for your children while trying to limit the number of disruptions, such as changing schools or changing child care. Consistency is key right now.

- Reassure your children that the divorce is *not* their fault. Explain that the change in living arrangements is a result of problems between you and your spouse, *not* between you (or your ex) and them.

- Let them know that you're there for them and are willing to discuss their fears and concerns.

- Don't sacrifice yourself completely for your children. You must *first* take care of yourself before you can take care of anyone else. Try to be a role model of self-esteem.

- Regularly reassure your children that you love them *no matter what.*

Obviously, each child may react somewhat differently to both the divorce and their new living arrangements. While no one can predict exactly how a child is going to respond, the age of the child can offer some clues.

Infants

While too young to understand the changes happening around them, having consistent routines will help your infants feel secure. Try to avoid changing naptimes, bedtimes, or feeding schedules. Most importantly, always remember to send their favorite toy or blanket when they're going from one parent's house to the other.

Toddlers

Typically, very young children are more likely to show regressive behavior. And while they *do* understand that one parent is not living at home anymore, they *don't* understand why. Expect lots of questions and know that even after everything has been explained (many times!), they probably still won't understand the answers. You may see increased whining and more difficulty making transitions. The best way to help your toddlers is to help them express their thoughts and feelings through language, play, and art. Art seemed to be a wonderful outlet for my kids when I was going through a divorce. Also, if you have the art interpreted by an accredited art therapist, it can provide great insight into unexpressed feelings your children may be experiencing.

Preschoolers

You may find your preschoolers becoming more fearful and anxious. Some might return to security blankets or stuffed animals or even experience lapses in toilet training. Don't be surprised by an increase in stomachaches and headaches during this time and possibly more sleeping problems. Socially, your preschoolers may become more apathetic—or more aggressive. Don't worry too much about these changes, but do keep an eye on them to make sure the changes are temporary. While most at this age are very confused by the changes in their lives, preschoolers also make an effort to try to understand the situation. In time, most do, and eventually learn to adjust well to their new environment.

Six- to eight-year-olds

This age group has a slightly better understanding of what divorce means. However, they often feel conflicted in their loyalties. If this is the case with your children, let them know it's *OK* to love and care for the other parent. Plus let them know it's OK to miss the other parent and want to be with them when they're not. Sometimes all it takes is getting "approval" from you to feel OK about their feelings and less conflicted about loving the other parent. Even with the approval, though, children of this age group still feel a deep sense of grief over the breakup of the family.

Nine- to twelve-year-olds

While trying to keep their emotions in check, this age group struggles with feelings of loss, embarrassment, and resentment. Perhaps the most intense emotion felt at this age is anger, and it's usually aimed at one parent or the other. Like most of the other ages, nine- to twelve-year-olds also experience new fears about their parents, such as where they are and when they'll see them next.

Twins have a unique advantage when dealing with divorce: *they have each other.* Don't ever underestimate how beneficial that bond can be when everything around them is changing. That's not to say that twins don't experience the same feelings any other kids would. It's just that twins have another bond to rely on, which is just as central to their lives as a parental bond. The twin bond provides them with a built-in support system that singletons just don't have. I was quite thankful to have twins when I was going through my divorce. Remember, my twins were quite young when this was happening in their lives. Just knowing that they had each other brought a sense of peace and calm amid the whirlwind of disruption.

How you can help

The best way you can help your children through any crisis is to be aware of any long-term significant changes in their usual pattern of behavior. While normal (and most typical) stress-related behaviors include becoming easily angered, trouble sleeping, a decline in school performance, or becoming withdrawn, keep an eye on the length of time each new behavior lasts. If you feel uncomfortable with what you see developing in your children or feel it's outside the range of what's normal, your children may benefit from outside help. The reality is that many children don't feel comfortable expressing negative feelings for fear of offending or angering either parent, or for fear of losing their love. Some children may feel safer discussing their feelings with a neutral party such as a therapist, grandparent, clergyperson, or teacher. Books can be helpful, too. A few that we liked are *My Parents Still Love Me Even Though They're Getting Divorced* by Lois V. Nightingale and *Dinosaurs Divorce* by Marc Brown and Laurene Krasny Brown. Both are written for four- to eight-year-olds, but other age-appropriate books are available. You never know what your children may respond to and it can, at the very least, open up a dialogue about divorce and their feelings about it.

Special needs and illness: how it affects the entire family

When parents are preparing for the arrival of their child(ren), the preparations rarely include dealing with the birth of a special needs child. Due to the higher percentage of premature births associated with twins, parents of twins must be more ready than others to deal with this reality. While the majority of preterm infants are born without major disabilities, there is a greater likelihood of significant health problems the earlier they're born, including lower birth weight. Whether you make the discovery at birth or many years later, the goal is always the same: to get your child the best possible help *and* to help other family members deal with the situation through understanding, love, and support. However, when the child with special needs is a twin, it adds a whole new level of complications. When one twin is physically, cognitively, or psychologically "different" from the other, both twins need reassurance that no one is at fault for the differences. Do expect anger and frustration from each twin, for different reasons.

The affected twin may experience feelings of "Why me?" and may be envious of her problem-free twin. The healthy twin may experience feelings of guilt, complicated by feelings of relief that she isn't like her twin. This can be very confusing. She may also feel jealous of the amount of time and attention given to her needier sibling.

As a parent, you must help each twin recognize his own strengths and limitations. Reassure your twins that their feelings are normal. Encourage them both to express their feelings as best they can. You can expect your own feelings to run the gamut from day to day, as well. After all, you and your spouse are also dealing with the broken fantasy of raising perfect kids. The good news is that most kids are resilient and, in time, are able to adjust to difficult situations. As long as you help them to feel safe, secure, and loved, they can survive just about anything. (By the way, *you* can, too.)

The death of a twin

While very little is known about the psychological impact of a twin's death on the surviving twin during infancy or early childhood, we do know that a child's grieving process is similar to an adult's. According to Eileen M. Pearlman, director of Twinsight, there will be many significant questions and issues to discuss depending on the age of the surviving twin. Some include:

- Why did I survive when my twin didn't?
- Am I still a twin?
- Did I cause my twin to die?
- I'll always miss what couldn't be and what we might have shared.
- I'll always wonder what my twin would have been like as an adult.

The greatest challenge for parents during this time is to help their child through the grieving process as they cope with their own loss. Acknowledge your twin's deep feelings of sadness and loss and try to answer his questions as honestly as possible. Accept that you and your child may grieve differently and will most likely process your emotions within different time frames. Most importantly, recognize that your child depends on you to take care of him and to help him understand and deal with his loss. Continually encourage him to express his feelings, thoughts, and fears. Understand that as your child's cognitive abilities develop, each stage will bring about additional fears, concerns, and questions.

Above all, make sure you are getting support for yourself. It will be impossible for you to meet the needs of your family if you're not taking care of yourself first.

Whether you choose professional help, a support group, a trusted family member, or your clergyperson, you need to find a comfortable outlet for your grief. Not only will you be helping yourself, you'll be helping your whole family in the long run.

Twin Types: Identicals vs. Fraternals

Identical twins

In order to understand the differences between the twin types, we must first understand the genesis of each. Identical twins, or monozygotic twins, are formed when a fertilized egg splits in half. Further splitting can occur, resulting in identical triplets, quadruplets, and more. What causes the fertilized egg to divide remains a mystery and many theories, such as delayed implantation of the fertilized egg in the uterus, or the time of fertilization, continue to be explored. Only one egg is involved; therefore, identical twins share 100 percent of their genes. Identical twins are always the same sex and have the same blood type. Boy/girl twins *cannot* be identical. You'd be amazed how many people don't know this. I can't tell you the number of times I've been asked if my boy/girl twins are identical. I used to answer this question with a lengthy biology lesson that usually resulted in the following response: "Duh, I *knew* that!" Now I just smile and say, "That's impossible," and let the other person ponder the reason why. It seems easier than making the other person feel . . . well, stupid. Also of interest is the fact that there is little evidence that identical twins are genetic. Identical twinning appears to occur at random, although the birth of more than one pair of identicals in some families has raised a few eyebrows and is worthy of further investigation. Some identical twins are referred to as "mirror image twins." An estimated 25 percent of identical twins show some form of mirror-image reversal (i.e., what you see when you look in the mirror), which most commonly shows up as opposite-handedness, hair whorls, dental features, and birthmarks.

Fraternal twins

Fraternal twins, or dizyogotic twins, are formed when two separate eggs are fertilized by two separate sperm. Fraternals share

50 percent of their genes and can either be the same sex or the opposite sex. Much more is understood about the causes of fraternal twins than identical twins, and two of the most common factors are a woman's age and her genetic predisposition. Besides age, did you know that the odds of having fraternal twins increase with maternal obesity and height? In the study mentioned in the introduction from *Obstetrics & Gynecology*, it was found that women with a body mass index (BMI) of 30 or more are significantly more likely to have fraternal twins than women with lower BMI's. The study also found that women who are in the twenty-fifth percentile of height increase their odds of having fraternal twins, although this association was not as strong as that for BMI. Now, for those of you with fraternal twins reading this, remain calm. The study does *not* say you must be obese to have fraternal twins. Nor does it say that you must be eye level with Shaq. It merely says that these issues *increase* the odds. That said, *I* have fraternal twins and I am only of average height and have actually been called scrawny once or twice in my life.

Typically, fraternal twinning occurs in women most often between the ages of thirty-five to thirty-nine. And unlike identicals, there is a tendency for fraternal twins to run in families. This genetic predisposition involves the tendency to release more than one egg at a time and obviously displays itself only through the mother. Now remember, the key word here is *typically.* My own situation was anything but typical. My fraternal twins were born when I was thirty-two, and the only twins in my family are *identical* great-uncles. If you don't fall neatly into the catalogue of characteristics linked to fraternal twinning, that's OK. There are actually many other factors linked to fraternal twins, including environmental issues and seasonality, to name a few. After my twins were born, the most common question I was asked (after "Are they identical?") was "Do twins run in your family?" Ironically, my answer was yes, but it had little to do with the fact that my twins were fraternal! Another common misconception about fraternals is that they "skip" a generation. While this may prove to be true in certain families, there is no evidence available to substantiate it.

Polar body twins

There is actually some evidence of a third twin type, called "polar body twinning," described as in between identicals and fraternals. They appear to be less alike than identical twins but more alike than fraternal twins and share 75 percent of their genes. Polar bodies occur when the primary egg divides twice on its way to maturity and is then fertilized by two separate sperm, yielding twins who typically share 100 percent of their mother's genes but only 50 percent of their father's genes. DNA testing is the only way to confirm polar body twins.

Conjoined twins

There is one additional subset of twins you've probably heard of: conjoined twins (often referred to as Siamese twins). Conjoined twins are formed when a fertilized egg begins to split but then stops partway, leaving the partially separated egg to mature into a conjoined fetus. This type of twinning is very rare and is more likely to occur in underdeveloped countries. While the cause of conjoined twins is unknown, the most common theory suggests a developmental delay in the splitting of the egg. But it is still unclear if this is due to genetic or environmental factors.

Even rarer twin types exist: chimerism is when fraternal twins are fused in utero, producing one individual with different sets of chromosomes; with superfecundation, the twins have different fathers; and with superfetation, eggs are released at different times, resulting in twins born days, weeks, or even months apart.

Twin development in utero

Now that you've learned about the biology of twinning, let's take it a step further. There seems to be much confusion about how twins actually develop in utero, and many wonder about the number of placentas involved, the intrauterine environment, the egg splitting, and so on. Here's some clarification for the curious: Fraternal twins each have their own separate placenta. In some situations, the placentas are implanted very close together and may fuse. This may give the appearance of *one* placenta when in actuality there are *two*. Estimates of fused placentas in fraternal twins are as high as 42 percent. Fraternals also have two chorions (outer membranes) and two amnions (inner membranes).

Identical twins are a bit more complicated. They may have one placenta or two, depending on when the egg splits. The earlier the split, the greater the likelihood there will be two placentas. Each placenta will have one chorion and one amnion. If the splitting occurs later (between day five and day seven), the placentas may fuse and there will be one chorion and two amnions. When the splitting occurs after day eight, typically there will be only one placenta, one chorion, and one amnion. Confused? Here's an easier way to sum it up: Fraternals almost always have two placentas (although they're sometimes fused) and identicals can either have one *or* two, depending on when the fertilized egg splits.

The influences of the intrauterine environment also have an impact on twins' development. These influences contribute to the theory that identicals are *not* identical in every way. Because of their different positions in the womb, one twin may have more room than the other, which may affect their growth. Placement in the womb may also affect what they hear, including the mother's voice and heartbeat. Plus, each twin receives their own nutrition, which may account for weight differences at birth.

A 1999 study conducted at the University of Milan considered the differences and the similarities in the intrauterine behavior of identical and fraternal twins. The behavior of fifteen identical twins and fifteen fraternal twins was studied through ultrasound between week ten and week twenty-two. The result? Each twin, regardless of its zygosity, showed *individual* behavior styles. While identical twins showed greater similarities in both activity and reactivity levels than fraternals, they were never behaviorally *identical,* and actually decreased in likeness with increasing age. In *all* the pairs, one twin was found to be more dominant, in the sense of being more active and less reactive. It was also determined that the differences each twin experienced in utero contributed to a progressively distinct behavior path for each.

Are identical twins identical in every way?

The short answer is no and the above study confirms it. In fact, the variations among twin types often make it hard for those closest to the twins (including the twins themselves) to know if they are identical or fraternal. In the introduction, you read about the importance of knowing the twin type (zygosity) of your children and learned about the methods available for finding out. But what accounts for the differences found in identical twins? Recent twin research suggests that these differences can be explained by lifestyle or environmental influences—both of which can have a real influence on DNA. As described in the Proceedings of the National Academy of Sciences, researchers measured the extent to which twins ranging in age from three to seventy-four differed in the number of genes that had either been turned on or shut down by certain biological mechanisms that influence gene activity. The results found that young twins had almost identical profiles, but that with age, their profiles became more and more divergent. In a finding that scientists are calling particularly groundbreaking, the profiles of twins who had been raised apart or who had different life experiences (including nutritional and exercise habits, history of illness, and use of alcohol, drugs, or tobacco), differed more than those twins who had lived together longer or who shared similar environments and experiences.

Also of interest is that smaller biological mechanisms that happen in utero most likely account for many of the minor distinguishing differences in the appearance, personality, and health of young identical twins (supporting the 1999 study mentioned above). What seems to be most exciting for geneticists, scientists, and researchers is that beyond its potential importance for understanding differences in identical twins, this field of research—called epigenetics—could explain many twists of fate that affect ordinary people. For instance, it may help us to understand why one person gets cancer and another doesn't. This type of research may hold the answer to one of biology's toughest questions: How do environmental influences such as exposure to certain pollutants or eating different foods produce lasting and potentially life-altering changes to our DNA? Twin studies are moving in exciting directions and allow us to explore both genetic and environmental influences on human development. The whole nature vs. nurture debate combined with this new type of research may help to explain many of the individual differences seen not only in twins, but also in the rest of us, for many years to come.

Twins, twins, everywhere?

The media's focus on twins would like us to believe that twins are everywhere. While there are more twins today than ever before due to sophisticated reproductive technology, the reality is there were only 125,134 twin deliveries in the United States in 2002. If identicals seem to be more plentiful than fraternals, it's only because their physical likeness makes them easier to spot. Most people assume that identical twins occur more frequently than fraternals. Not true. Among Caucasians, identical twins represent only about one-third of all twin births while fraternals represent the other two-thirds of the twin population.. Another interesting tidbit: while the identical twinning rate remains fairly constant across other populations and ethnic groups, the fraternal twinning rate radically fluctuates. Fraternal twins among Asian populations remain low, while just the opposite is true in some African populations. In fact, Nigeria has the highest twinning rate in the world. In western Nigeria's Yoruba tribe, one out of every eleven persons is a twin.

The twin bond: does it differ between twin types?

Let's get a few things straight. While the twin bond is an unusually strong one, twins do not have ESP; nor are they clones. Other myths abound. A few to clarify: not all twins are best friends; the "good twin/evil twin" theory is completely without merit; and no, twins do not always act the same—even identicals. That said, identical twins are *more* inclined to be close than fraternals, and girls are generally more attached to each other than boys. Identicals also tend to be more aware of and more cooperative with each other than fraternals. In addition, because identicals share the same genes and chromosomes, they're more likely to have similar interests and temperaments. The reality is, no matter what the twin type, the twin bond is like no other and the quality of the bond tends to vary; some twins have a very close bond, while others do not. Many twins are also very competitive with each other. The ever popular question "Who's older?" is usually a dreaded one. While my own twins are only one minute apart, I made a point not to tell them for many years. Every minute becomes increasingly significant to the "older" twin as he relishes his seniority over the "younger" twin. No need to add fuel to the fire.

Boy/girl twins

Until recently, researchers preferred to study the similarity of identical twins in comparison to same-sex fraternals, leaving opposite-sex twins in the dust. Not anymore. There seems to be a newfound interest in studying gender-related behavioral differences to learn the variations in how males and females function. Some of these research opportunities have produced captivating ideas and findings. A few examples: one researcher studied sensation seeking (the desire for thrill and adventure), a behavior in which males usually outscore females. Her study was able to show that females from opposite-sex pairs scored higher in this type of behavior than females from same-sex pairs. Another study found that while males typically outperform females on some spatial-ability tasks, this is not true with opposite-sex twins. Female twins were on par with their twin brothers and obtained higher initial scores than same-sex fraternal twins. Yet another study revealed that a coed fetal environment offered protection against fetal and newborn death as well as brain damage due to oxygen deficiency at birth. All of these findings highlight the importance of continued focus on both behavioral and environmental differences among opposite-sex twins.

To sum it up

While the behavioral differences found in fraternal twins can be explained by both genetic and environmental factors, the differences found in identical twins can be explained only by environmental factors. But there's so much more to learn. This is a very exciting time for twin researchers, as current advances in genetics allow them to study twins like never before.

No matter what type of twins you have: identical girls or boys, fraternal girls or boys, or opposite-sex twins, cherish and value their unique, lifelong bond. Celebrate their differences as well as their similarities and know you're witnessing a fascinating study in human development on a daily basis.

This Ain't So Bad Now (Till Adolescence, That Is)

In chapter one, you read about the necessity of childproofing *before* your twins were walking. Hopefully, you've learned to be proactive in each new stage of your twins' development. Well, it's that time again, but on an entirely new level. As your twins enter the preteens years, you're living in the calm before the storm. Life with your family has probably fallen into a more predictable routine and you may actually have time to put your feet up every now and then. Better yet, your twins are well on their way to self-sufficiency. What a relief from the early years of double duty! The degree of active participation in your twins' life has changed dramatically, too. For some, this change represents a new sense of freedom in their own lives. For others, it brings mixed feelings. Many parents may not feel as needed in their twins' lives and have a hard time letting go. But doesn't this happen with every stage? I remember feeling that way when my kids finished toilet training and when they started kindergarten. Every developmental milestone makes you realize how quickly time goes by. Plus, each stage brings its own set of joys and difficulties. This stage is no different. You're just dealing with different issues. Don't be fooled into thinking your twins no longer need you. You've helped them build their foundations since birth. You can hardly stop now! Especially with adolescence hot on your heels. For now, relish the calm. Sooner than you think, you'll be dealing with the bigger-than-life issues of adolescence. Now's the time to prepare yourself and your kids for what's ahead.

Make sure the lines of communication are open

Even though this seems like a relatively calm time, your twins still have a lot going on. Make sure they know they can come to you, or your partner, to have their questions answered about *anything.* Some kids may be on the verge of reaching puberty, and their changing bodies leave them feeling self-conscious and confused. Typically, girls experience these changes first; but, as with everything else in child development, the range is extremely wide. As your twins get closer to approaching middle school, they'll have an increased desire to fit in. And any bodily changes they've experienced can make for some pronounced differences. Those differences can be especially noticeable in your own two. Not long ago, my daughter experienced a colossal growth spurt and grew an astonishing four inches in three months. My son, who was rolling along at a normal pace, (and who, by the way, has always been *above* average in height) one day looked at his sister and said, "My God, you're *so* tall!" While we all just looked at each other and burst out laughing, there wasn't a doubt in my mind that what he really meant to say was, "You're so tall, *what happened to me?*" To add to his dispirit were well-intentioned friends commenting on the height difference between them: "Don't worry Evan, you'll catch up soon. You'll probably be taller than she is one day." One look at Evan's face told me he'd rather have his eyes poked with sharp needles than listen to direct comparisons of him and his sister. I can't say I blame him. The competition between twins is pretty fierce at this stage. The last thing they need is for people to point out different physical characteristics between them, especially when they're feeling so self-conscious about it. The challenge for you during this time is to provide support to both children. Between the hormones kicking in, the radical growth spurts, and curiosity about life after elementary school, there is a big fear of the unknown. Let your children know you're there for them no matter what.

Parenting preteens

Take a good look at your twins right now, and you might be surprised at what you see. While you've been busy tending to all their needs over the years, you may not have noticed that they've developed some pretty amazing qualities along the way. They are probably more self-assured than ever before as they begin to develop a stronger sense of self. And they're certainly more vocal. Their language skills have become much more sophisticated. Not only are they able to vocalize their likes and dislikes (and quite *loudly*, I might add), they are able to back up their opinions through reasoning and logic. If you listen closely enough, you'll be able to learn how each twin views the world around them—not to mention how each processes the information they receive. I love to hear my twins describe the same experience *completely* differently. It gives me great insight into how their minds work, as well as to what's important to them. Plus, it teaches me how to give information to each of them to make sure I get the response I need. Your twins are probably also becoming more organized and dependable, which is the beginning of greater independence for all of you.

When twins become preteens, they want to be seen as individuals and will work extra hard at staking out their own territory. As their worlds continue to grow, they will probably begin to be less dependent on one another. Each is developing the social skills to stand on their own. Of course, this seldom happens at the same time. You may have one with a greater need for separateness than the other. Or, they may exhibit differences in ability (academically or physically). Your job is to figure out how to support the needs of each without diminishing the other. As they continue through this stage, you must often "adjust" how you relate to them. In many ways, this is a positive change. The relationship between you and your twins is slowly evolving into a more mature one.

This is also a time when the differences between both the twin types *and* the sexes begin to stand out more. Fraternals may become less alike; identicals may begin comparing everything down to the smallest detail, and same-sex twins become more aware of each other's physical characteristics. But, opposite-sex multiples may exhibit the most exaggerated differences of all—for obvious reasons. A case in point is the height difference between my two. Pay close attention to the dynamic between your twins and don't be surprised by the growing pains they may be experiencing. Your twins are well on their way to becoming independent, self-sufficient little people. You can pat yourself on the back for a job well done.

Into adolescence

As your twins wind their way into early adolescence, many challenges lie ahead for all of you. Twins who have always been close may find themselves separating much more right now. As with every stage in life, the ebb and flow of their relationship is evolving and maturing. While the basis for identity formation occurs from birth to age two, the final throes occur in adolescence. They may find themselves having to do extra work to emotionally separate from their twin.

All children have environments to which they must adapt. The only child has a specific environment—as does the firstborn. Twins are no different. However, their environment involves coming into this world *together* instead of by themselves. Plus, they have twin myths, twin stereotypes, and twin expectations to deal with. At their age, this is a lot to handle. The best thing you can do for your twins is to step back and allow them the space they need to redefine their relationship. Trust them and believe they will adjust as needed, in their own way.

On the flip side, the good news is that twins have the added benefit of sharing adolescence and having company at a time when many teenagers are feeling particularly isolated. Depending on how your twins relate to one another, you may find them turning to each other instead of you. Don't fret. Consider yourself lucky that they have someone to talk to. Also note that they may begin to relate more to the same-sex parent as they get closer to adolescence. This is a wonderful opportunity for you and your partner to explore new territory with each twin. Take advantage of this time by sharing in gender-related activities. It's important to do whatever it takes to stay connected to your twins as they surge toward adulthood.

Movin' on

It seems like just yesterday your twins were infants: innocent, dependent, and so very brand-new. Often when I think of my own twins, the first image that pops into my head is one of younger days. Don't be surprised at the range of emotions you may experience as your twins enter this new phase. Especially when you think of all the trials and tribulations you've been through to get to this point. Some parents mourn the earlier years of childhood while others, myself included, relish their twins' burgeoning independence. It all depends on your perspective. There are days when I look at my twins and am amazed at who they've become. Both are smart, sensitive, kind, and have the greatest sense of humor. Not a day goes by in my house when we're not laughing hysterically—with tears streaming down our faces—over silly things. Often it's the *best* part of my day. It's times like these that have helped to create an intense bond between the three of us. As they grow and mature, I find myself turning to them more and more for their knowledge, opinions, and input.

Take Evan, for instance. His computer knowledge rivals Bill Gates's and he has literally saved my ass on many different occasions. With three computers networked in my house, a computer crisis is a daily occurrence. I can't tell you how many times he has helped me locate a lost document or guided me through the simplest of problems *without* making me feel like an idiot. Once he actually saved my hard drive from crashing, and *me* from almost having a nervous breakdown because of it. Plus, he did so with the utmost grace and aplomb. Nothing is better than having a live-in computer techie on call 24/7—and the price is right, to boot. Maya, on the other hand, is the one

I turn to when I need to brainstorm creative solutions to complicated problems. She is the best "outside the box" thinker I've ever met and has helped me out of many conundrums. As I said in the beginning of this book, my twins make me proud to be their mother. I'm happy to say nothing has changed through the years (although talk to me again after adolescence—I may have a whole new perspective and, perhaps, a sequel on its horrors . . .). All kidding aside, life is filled with ups and downs—twins or no twins. This next phase is no different. Just make sure you're as prepared as you can be for the bumps along the way—you will, no doubt, definitely hit some. While I've often wished parenthood came with an instruction manual, muddling through has seemed to work just fine. I have no doubt this philosophy will carry my family through adolescence as well. On the days that you feel doubly cursed instead of doubly blessed, remember, tomorrow's a new day. Day to day is just about the best *any* of us can do.

You've come a long way. Continue to love your twins and cherish each and every day with them, even when confronted with the pot, booze, crashed car, or failing report card (sorry for the harsh reality check). Always remember, they're depending on *you* to set them straight. When I look at my friends who are sending their kids to college already, I feel a twinge of sadness. Well, actually I feel like I've been punched in the stomach. Raising twins is a gift. All too quickly, they're out the door and you're left to wonder how it went by so quickly. While you're not there quite yet, it never hurts to be prepared. In the meantime, carry on as best you can and go easy on yourself. Expect a wild ride and rejoice when life goes more smoothly than you expected. Make sure to have some fun along the way, but don't ever let your twins forget who's boss. Most importantly, at the end of the day, the best thing you can do is to let your twins know you love them unconditionally. And all this time you thought raising twins was hard work.

Resources

TWIN-SPECIFIC

Australian Multiple Birth Association (AMBA)
P.O. Box 105
Coogee, N.S.W., 2034 Australia
(011) (612) 6971-2805
www.amba.org.au

Center for Loss in Multiple Birth (CLIMB)
P.O. Box 91377
Anchorage, AK 99509
(907) 222-5321
www.climb-support.org

The Center for the Study of Multiple Birth (CSMB)
333 E. Superior St., Suite 464
Chicago, IL 60611
(312) 695-1677
www.multiplebirth.com

International Society for Twin Studies (ISTS)
Queensland Institute of Medical Research
Post Office, Royal Brisbane Hospital
Brisbane, QLD 4029, Australia
www.ists.qimr.edu.au

Irish Multiple Births Association (IMBA)
P.O. Box 5053
Swords
Co. Dublin, Ireland
homepages.iol.ie/~erogers/imba.htm

Mothers of Supertwins (MOST)
P.O. Box 306
East Islip, NY 11730
(631) 859-1110
www.MOSTonline.org

Multiple Births Canada
P.O. Box 432
Wasaga Beach, Ontario
Canada L9Z 1A4
(705) 429-0901
www.multiplebirthscanada.org

National Organization of Mothers of Twins Clubs, Inc (NOMOTC)

P.O. Box 700860
Plymouth, Michigan 48170
(877) 540-2200
www.nomotc.org

New Zealand Multiple Birth Association (NZMBA)

P.O. Box 1258
Wellington, New Zealand
www.nzmba.info

The Twins Foundation

P.O. Box 6043
Providence, RI 02940
(401) 751-TWIN
www.twinsfoundation.com

Twinstuff.com

P.O. Box 395
Missouri City, TX 77489
(832) 212-4793
www.twinstuff.com

The Twin to Twin Transfusion Syndrome Foundation

411 Longbeach Parkway
Bay Village, OH 44140
(800) 815-9211
www.tttsfoundation.org

Twinless Twins Support Group

P.O. Box 980481
Ypsilanti, MI 48198
(888) 205-8962
www.twinlesstwins.org

Twinsight

1137 Second St., Suite 109
Santa Monica, CA 90403
(310) 458-1373
www.twinsight.com

***Twins* Magazine**

11211 E. Arapahoe Rd., Suite 101
Centennial, CO 80112
(888) 55-TWINS
www.twinsmagazine.com

Twins Days Festival
P.O. Box 29
Twinsburg, OH 44087
(330) 425-3652
www.twinsdays.org

Twins and Multiple Births Association (TAMBA) - United Kingdom
2 The Willows
Gardner Road
Guildford, Surrey, England
GU1 4PG
(011) (44) 870-770-3305
www.tamba.org.uk

HEALTH, SAFETY, AND EDUCATION

American Academy of Child and Adolescent Psychiatry
3615 Wisconsin Ave., N.W.
Washington, D.C. 20016
(202) 966-7300
www.aacap.org

American Academy of Pediatrics
141 Northwest Point Blvd.
Elk Grove Village, IL 60007
(847) 434-4000
www.aap.org

American Speech-Language-Hearing Association (ASHA)
10801 Rockville Pike
Rockville, MD 20852
(800) 638-8255
www.asha.org

Attention Deficit Disorder Resources
223 Tacoma Ave. S., #100
Tacoma, WA 98402
(253) 759-5085
www.addresources.org

Autism Society of America
7910 Woodmont Ave., Suite 300
Bethesda, MD 20814
(800) 3-AUTISM
www.autism-society.org

The Child Advocate

www.childadvocate.net

Centers for Disease Control and Prevention (CDC)

1600 Clifton Rd.

Atlanta, GA 30333

(404) 639-3311

www.cdc.gov

Learning Disabilities Association of America

4156 Library Rd.

Pittsburgh, PA 15234

(412) 341-1515

www.ldanatl.org

National Education Association

1201 16th St., N.W.

Washington, D.C. 20036

(202) 833-4000

www.nea.org

National Mental Health Association

2001 N. Beauregard St., 12th floor
Alexandria, VA 22311
(703) 684-7722
www.nmha.org

National Resource Center for Health and Safety in Child Care

UCHSC at Fitzsimons
Campus Mail Stop F541; P.O. Box 6508
Aurora, CO 80045
(800) 598-KIDS
http://nrc.uchsc.edu

Parents Without Partners

1650 South Dixie Highway, Suite 510
Boca Raton, FL 33432
www.parentswithoutpartners.org

Proactive Genetics

525 Blackburn Drive
Martinez, GA 30907
(866) TWINS-DNA
www.proactivegenetics.com

SHARE: Pregnancy and Infant Loss Support

St. Joseph Health Center

300 First Capitol Drive

St. Charles, MO 63301

(800) 821-6819

www.nationalshareoffice.com

Acknowledgments

I'd like to thank the following people for their love, support and encouragement: Elaine Gottesman, George Gottesman, Jeanne Cribbs, Nancy Gottesman, Carel Deioungh, Robby Gottesman, Rick Gottesman, Eve Gottesman, Danny Gottesman, Matthew Gottesman, David Kemper, Tracy Lincenberg, Caren Berg, Jill Rosen, Kelli Benson, Diana Hurst, and Brett Grodeck.

A very sincere thank you to the twin "experts," Dr. Nancy L. Segal, professor of psychology at the University of California, Fullerton, and Eileen M. Pearlman, director of Twinsight, for their time and expertise.

Grateful acknowledgement goes to the many parents of twins, too numerous to name, who so willingly shared their stories with me and allowed me to share them with you.

Thanks and gratitude to Sue McCloskey, Matthew Lore, Peter Jacoby, and the entire Marlowe staff for their ongoing patience, support, and professionalism. Truly a wonderful team to work with.

Finally, thanks and infinite love to my own personal "lab rats," Maya and Evan, for making this book, and everything else, possible.

INDEX

A

AACAP (American Academy of Child & Adolescent Psychiatry), 102–103, 106–107
AAP (American Academy of Pediatrics), 72, 107–108, 111–112
academics
  in fifth grade, 197
  in fourth grade, 196–197
  preschool and, 53
activities, charitable, 210–212
activities, extracurricular, 180–185
activities, separate vs. together. *See* separate activities vs. keeping them together
adolescence, 238–239
affection period, 166–167
aggression
  attention and, 98–100
  biting, 40–41
  fighting, 45, 134–135, 187
  self-control, 99
  temper tantrums, 35–38
airplane travel, 71–77
American Academy of Child & Adolescent Psychiatry (AACAP), 102–103, 106–107
American Academy of Pediatrics (AAP), 72, 107–108, 111–112
American Heart Association, 110–112
American Speech-Language-Hearing Association, 25
Ames, Louise Bates, 12
anti-affection stage, 166
antibacterial hand sanitizer, 91
anxiety in children
  in four-year-olds, 100–101
  and middle school, transition to, 198
  in second graders, 175–176
  separation anxiety and preschool, 56–59
anxiety in parents
  developmental stages and, 12–13
  preschool and, 55–57
  work and, 162
art therapy, 219
attention. *See also* competition and rivalry
  aggression and, 98–100
  from curious classmates, 189–190
  jealousy and, 106
  pretend sickness for, 92–93
  to reinforce good behavior, 42
authority, enforcing, 41
autonomous language (cryptophasia), 23, 84–86
autonomy. *See* independence and autonomy

B

baby pictures, separate, 16
babysitters, 49, 147
Baker, Sidney, 12
bargaining, 95
battles, picking, 36
bed of parents, reclaiming, 147–148
behavioral differences
  gender-related, 233–234
  normal and abnormal behavior, 201–202
  in utero, 229–230

behavior reinforcement. *See* reinforcement of good behavior
biblical twins, 2
birthday cakes, 16
birthday parties, 171–174
birth order, 233
birth rate of twins, 5–7, 8, 232
biting, 40–41
bond of twins. *See* closeness and bond of twins
books and reading, 24, 65
brain wave patterns, 8
Brazelton, T. Berry, 9, 52
Brown, Laurene Krasny, 220
Brown, Marc, 220
budgeting, 154

C
car seats, 72, 79
car travel, 77–78
charitable activities, 210–212
childproofing
  homes, 12, 18–20
  hotels, 78
child-safety seats, 72, 79
chimerism, 228
choice given to toddlers, 42
classroom placement, separate vs. together, 118–129, 186
closeness and bond of twins. *See also* individuality, individuation, and separation
  adolescence and, 238–239
  as built-in support system, 220
  fighting and, 134
  gender and, 232
  independent decision making and, 138
  schools and, 126
  singleton sibling and, 140
  twin language and, 84–86
  unbreakability of, 33
  variations in, 233
  zygosity and, 4, 232–233
clothes
  change of, when traveling, 76–77
  dressing differently vs. alike, 14–15
  self-dressing and toilet training, 61
clubs for parents of twins, 17–18, 43–44
COBRA insurance, 154
communication
  child behavior as, 201–202
  in marriage, 144–145
  in preteen years, 235–237
comparison
  competitiveness and, 137
  developmental stages and, 13
  homework and, 185–186
  puberty and, 236, 238
  at school, 121
  school, talking about, 195–196
  self-esteem and, 39–40
competition and rivalry
  attention and, 131–132
  extracurricular activities and, 182
  fighting, 45, 134–135
  friendly contests, 117–118
  homework and, 186, 187
  how to help, 135–138
  parental attitudes and individuality, 132–134
  puberty and, 236
  scenarios and stories, 140–142
  with singleton siblings, 139–140
  toilet training and, 62
  "who's older," 233
complaints, 194–195
compliments, 95
computers, 206–210
conjoined twins, 227–228
consistency

divorce and, 217
parenting styles and, 146
with toddlers, 41
copying each other
in play, 14
profanity and, 89
toilet training and, 62
corner covers, 19
crises, 215–216, 220
crushes, 204, 206
cryptophasia, 23, 84–86

D

dads, stay-at-home, 160
date night for parents, 147
day care vs. preschool, 49
death of a twin, 222–223
decision making, independent, 138
dependence on each other. *See also* closeness and bond of twins
identicals vs. fraternals, 4, 108, 232–233
placement together at school and, 120
shifting balances in, 133
developmental stages
at 1 year of age, 13–14
at 2 years of age ("terrible twos"), 31–32
at 3 years of age, 47–48, 52
at 4 years of age, 88–90, 96
at 5 years of age, 105–106, 107
at 6 to 8 years of age, 166–168
at 9 and 10 years of age, 193–194, 198–199
anxiety about, 12–13
preschool and, 52
preteen years and adolescence, 235–242
speech and language, 22–28, 86, 237
timing differences in twins, 13, 48, 61–62, 188–189, 199
toilet training and, 68–69
walking, 20–22
development in utero, 228–230
diapers, 76
Dinosaurs Divorce (Brown and Brown), 220
disability, 215–216
discipline, 101–104
discounts, 73, 185
disequilibrium, 32
distractedness and homework, 187
divorce, 142–144, 216–220
dizygotic twins. *See* fraternal (dizygotic) twins
DNA analysis, 5
doctor. *See* pediatrician, consulting with
dressing differently vs. alike, 14–15
dressing themselves and toilet training, 61
driving, 180

E

ear pain on airplanes, 77
eating out, 80–84
embarrassment, 170–171
embryonic development, 228–230
emotional distancing, 166–167
emotions and the "terrible twos," 33–37
empathy, development of, 167
epigenetics, 231
equal time, 16–17
equitable vs. equal, 137
Everyone Poops (Gomi), 65
exercise, 115–118
expectations
at 9 and 10 years of age, 198–199
eating out and, 80–82
school and, 189

experts and advice, 8–9, 50
extracurricular activities, 180–185

F
FAA (Federal Aviation Administration), 72
fantasy, 96–97
fascination with twins, 2–3
favoritism, 136–137
fears
 divorce and, 219
 in four-year-olds, 100–101
 in second graders, 175–176
Federal Aviation Administration (FAA), 72
fertility technology, 7
fighting. *See also* aggression
 homework and, 187
 as normal, 134
 story about, 45
 when to intervene, 134–135
financial security issues, 154
fingerprints, 8
flex-time work, 156–157
flu, 93
follicle-stimulating hormone (FSH), 7
food
 eating out, 80–84
 healthy nutrition habits, 109–115
 junk food, 113, 170
 picky eaters, 113–114
 snacks with visiting friends, 170
 for traveling, 76, 79
Frankel, Alona, 65
fraternal (dizygotic) twins
 birth rate, 232
 closeness of, 4
 genesis of, 224–225
 genetic predisposition, 225–226
 meaning of, 3–4
 puberty and physical differences, 238
 in utero development, 228–230
friends, imaginary, 97
friendships
 in 3rd grade, 176–177
 in 5th grade, 199–201
 birthday parties of friends, 171
 learning about, 168–169
 tips for helping with, 169–171
 twin status, exploitation of, 189–190
 the "wrong crowd," 200
FSH (follicle-stimulating hormone), 7

G
gemellology, 7
gender-related behavioral differences, 233–234. *See also* opposite-sex twins
genetic predisposition to twinning, 225–226
germs and illness. *See* illness
gifts, birthday, 173
Gomi, Taro, 65
grandparents, 136
grieving process, 222–223
growth spurts, 236

H
hand washing, 91
hazards and childproofing, 18–20
headaches, 195, 219
health
 exercise, 115–118
 illness, 90–94, 220–222
 nutrition habits, 109–115
 pain relievers, 77
 stomachache/headache excuse, 195
 zygosity and medical issues, 4
health insurance, 153–154
height differences, 236, 238

height of mother and birth rate of fraternal twins, 225
help, asking for, 17–18, 43–44
higher-order multiples, rate of birth of, 7, 8
homework, 185–188, 197
hotels, 78–80
humor, sense of, 37
hurts, 100–101

I

identical (monozygotic) twins
- birth rate, 232
- closeness of, 4
- dependence on each other, 108
- differences in, 230–231
- genesis of, 223–224
- meaning of, 3–4
- mirror image twins, 224
- puberty and, 238
- telling them apart, 15
- in utero development, 229–230

identities, evolution of, 166–167. *See also* individuality, individuation, and separation
idioglossia, 23, 84–86
Ilg, Frances, 12
illness, 90–94, 220–222. *See also* health
imaginary friends, 97
imagination, 96–97
IM (instant messaging), 208, 209
immunizations, 91–92
inactivity, physical, 115–116
independence and autonomy. *See also* dependence on each other
- at 9 and 10 years of age, 198
- decision making and, 138
- during "terrible twos," 32–33, 34
- walking and, 21

individuality, individuation, and separation. *See also* closeness and bond of twins; separate activities vs. keeping them together
- at 1 year of age, 14–16
- at 4 years of age, 94–95
- at 9 and 10 years of age, 193–194
- in adolescence, 238–239
- biting and, 40
- competition and, 132–134
- dressing differently, 14–15
- praising their individuality, 138
- preschool and separation anxiety, 56–59
- preteens and, 237–238
- telling identical twins apart, 15
- "terrible twos" and, 33
- in utero, 229–230

infant elimination training, 59–60
injury, 100–101
intelligence, 188
interdependence. *See* closeness and bond of twins; dependence on each other
interests, natural development of, 181–182
Internet safety, 206–210
intrauterine behavior, 229–230
in utero development, 228–230
IQ tests, 188

J

jealousy, 106, 200
job-sharing, 157–158
journaling, 37
junk food, 113, 170

K

kindergarten, readiness for, 106–109. *See also* school
Kissing Hand, The (Penn), 109

L

labeling, 133

language development. *See* speech and language
lap restraint systems, 73
Leeper, Sarah H., 128
lifestyle habits
- exercise, 115–118
- nutrition, 109–115

limit setting and temper tantrums, 36
love, enough to go around, 44

M

marriage
- conflict, potential causes of, 144–146
- divorce, 142–144, 216–220
- making time for spouse, 146–149, 161
- professional help, 149
- and work, decision to return to, 158

marriage counseling, 149
middle school, transition to, 198, 203
mimicking. *See* copying each other
mirror image twins, 224
modeled behavior, 103
monozygotic twins. *See* identical (monozygotic) twins
moral development, 198–199
multiples, higher order, birth rate of, 7, 8
My Parents Still Love Me Even Though They're Getting Divorced (Nightingale), 220
mythological twins, 2

N

nagging and toilet training, 64
National Health and Nutrition Examination (NHANES), 110
National Institute on Deafness and Other Communication Disorders (NIDCD), 25
National Organization of Mothers of Twins Clubs, Inc. (NOMOTC)
- on classroom placement, 119–121, 125, 126, 128
- on divorce, 144
- as source of support, 43

NHANES (National Health and Nutrition Examination), 110
NIDCD (National Institute on Deafness and Other Communication Disorders), 25
Nightingale, Lois V., 220
"no," 33
NOMOTC. *See* National Organization of Mothers of Twins Clubs, Inc.
nutrition habits, healthy, 109–115. *See also* food

O

obesity of children and teens, 110–111
obesity of mothers, 225
"older" twin, 233
Once Upon a Potty (Frankel), 65
opposite-sex twins
- gender-related behavioral differences, 233–234
- privacy and, 191
- puberty and physical differences, 236, 238
- separate friends and, 171

out-of-bounds behavior by four-year-olds, 94–95
overweight children and teens, 110–111

P

pain, anticipation of, 101
pain relievers, 77
parallel play, 14
parenting style differences, 144, 146

parties, birthday, 171–174
part-time work, 153, 156–157
patience and toilet training, 59, 64
Pearlman, Eileen M., 85, 222
pediatrician, anxiety about visits to, 101
pediatrician, consulting with
  on developmental concerns, 13, 88
  health history, knowing, 91
  on immunizations, 91–92
  on language development, 24–25
  on toilet training, 67–68
peers, influence of, 199–201. *See also* friendships
Penn, Audrey, 109
"perfect" child-rearing, 9
personality development, 47–48. *See also* individuality, individuation, and separation
pharmacies, 91
photographs, separate, 16
physical activity, 115–118
picky eaters, 113–114
"pick your battles," 36
pictures, separate, 16
Placement of Multiple Birth Children in School (NOMOTC), 119–121, 126
placentas, 228, 229
play
  at 1 year of age, 14
  eating out, toys for, 83
  extracurricular activities, 180–185
  preschool and, 55–56
  traveling, toys for, 75, 77–78
playdates, 169–170
polar body twins, 227
pools, 19–20, 79
positive reinforcement. *See* reinforcement of good behavior
potty training. *See* toilet training
power change in marriage relationships, 145
power struggles, 36, 63
pregnant with twins, getting the news, 151
preschool, 47–59
  choosing the right one, 53–55
  day care vs., 49
  parental anxiety about, 55–56
  as personal decision, 49–50
  readiness for, 50–52
  separation anxiety, 56–59
  socialization and, 47–48, 53
preteen years, 212–213, 235–242
privacy, 191
profanity, 89–90
puberty, 236–237
Pull-Ups, 66

Q

questions
  asked by adults, 3
  asked by kids, 190
  "why" (from twins), 98
  quitting, 184–185

R

Raising Charitable Children Survey, 210
reading and books, 24, 65
reasoning skills, 198–199
reflection, 88
regressive behavior, 67–68, 218–219
reinforcement of good behavior
  "terrible twos" and, 42
  toilet training and, 63, 64, 66, 67
rental cars, 79
repetitive behavior in toddlers, 38–39. *See also* copying each other
reproductive technology, 7

restaurants, 80–84
rewards. *See* reinforcement of good behavior
ritualistic behavior in toddlers, 38–39
rivalry. *See* competition and rivalry
rules
 for computer use, 207, 208–210
 discipline for 4-year-olds, 101–102
 for fighting, 135
 friends visiting and, 170
Russell, Jean M., 127

S

same-sex twins
 mimicking by, 62
 mutual friends of, 171
 study preference for, 233
schedules and overscheduling, 180–181
school. *See also* preschool
 first graders, 174–175
 second graders, 175–176
 third graders, 176–177
 fourth graders, 196–197
 fifth graders, 197–198, 202–203
 curious classmates, 189–190
 extracurricular activities, 180–185
 helping them open up about, 178–179, 195–196
 homework, 185–188
 middle school, 198, 203
 placing separately or together, 118–129, 186
 readiness for, 106–109
 success, encouraging, 188–189
 support, academic, 196–197
 volunteering at, 177–178
Sears, William, 9
seatbelts, 73
secret language, 23, 84–86
security checkpoints in airports, 74–75
Segal, Nancy L., 4, 127
self-control, 99, 103, 174
self-esteem
 comparison and, 39–40
 letting each know they are special, 138
 "terrible twos" emotional rollercoaster and, 34
self-expression in four-year-olds, 89–90, 95, 96
separate activities vs. keeping them together. *See also* individuality, individuation, and separation
 alone time, 138
 classroom placement, 118–129, 186
 equal time and, 16–17
 photographs, 16
 preschool and, 50–51
separation anxiety and preschool, 56–59
sex education, 204–206
sexes, opposite. *See* opposite-sex twins
sharing and play, 14
Siamese (conjoined) twins, 227–228
sibling rivalry. *See* competition and rivalry
siblings, singleton, 139–140
sickness, 90–94, 220–222. *See also* health
single parenting, benefits of, 149–150
singletons, 5, 139–140
Skipper, Dora S., 128
socialization
 birthday parties, 171–174
 controlling aggression and, 99
 in fifth grade, 197
 preschool and, 47–48, 53
socially conscious kids, 210–212
special needs children, 215–216, 220–222
speech and language

cryptophasia (twin language), 23, 84–86
development of, 22–28, 86
preschool and, 54
in preteens, 237
profanity, 89–90
silly language, 95
Spock, Benjamin, 9, 10
sports, 183, 184–185
stages of development. *See* developmental stages
stay-at-home dads, 160
stomachaches, 195, 219
stomach flu, 93
stress-related behaviors, 220
superfecundation, 228
superfetation, 228
supervision around water, 20
superwoman, quest to be, 155–156
support groups, 17–18, 43–44
support system and working, 160–161
swearing, 89–90
swimming pools, 19–20, 79

T

table corners, 19
tag-team effect
discipline and, 103–104
"terrible twos" and, 35
toilet training and, 63
taking care of yourself first, 44
tantrums, 35–38, 42
teachers
comparison by, 121
in fifth grade, 197
in first grade, 174, 175
observing interaction with, 178
in preschool, 54, 55, 58, 162
and separation of twins, 118, 123, 124–125
staying in touch with, 179
twin tricks played on, 122
team sports, 183, 184–185
teasing, 206
teenagers, overweight, 111
teeth, losing, 174–175
television, 175–176
temperament in four-year-olds, 94–95
temper tantrums, 35–38, 42
terminology, 3–5
"terrible twos," 31–38
time issues
alone time with each, 135–136
apart time, 138, 191
equitable division of time, 16–17
extracurricular activities and, 180–181, 183
language development and, 23, 24
spouse, time for, 145, 146–149, 161
yourself, time for, 44
time-outs, 102
Timothy Goes to School (Wells), 109
together vs. separate. *See* separate activities vs. keeping them together
toilet training, 59–69
do's and don'ts, 63–65
infant elimination training, 59–60
patience and, 59, 64
pee targets, 68
preschool requirements for, 53
process with twins, 61–63
stories from moms on, 66–68
timing and readiness, 59, 60–61, 63, 68–69
underwear vs. Pull-Ups, 66, 68
toys
for eating out, 83
for traveling, 75, 77–78

Transportation Security Administration (TSA), 74–75
traveling
by airplane, 71–77
by car, 77–78
hotels, 78–80
triangle relationships, 139–140, 169
trick playing by twins, 122
TSA (Transportation Security Administration), 74–75
twin, origin of term, 8
twin language, 23, 84–86
Twins in the Classroom (Segal and Russell), 127
twin type. *See* zygosity

U

ultrasound, 5, 29
underwear and toilet training, 66–67

V

vanishing twins, 5
VCRs, 19
video cameras, 29
volunteering at school, 177–178

W

walking, 20–22
weekend getaways, 148–149
weight and overweight children, 110–111
weight of mother and birth rate of fraternal twins, 225
Wells, Rosemary, 109
"why," 98
window blind strings, 19
working parents
"be ready for anything," 162–163
decision to return to work, 151–158
financial security issues, 154
health insurance and, 153–154
job-sharing, 157–158
nine-to-five issues, 158–162
part-time or flex-time, 153, 156–157
personal identity issues, 154–155
preschool and, 49
sick children and, 92
stats on, 152–153
superwoman, quest to be, 155–156
working from home, 157

Z

zygosity (twin type). *See also* identical (monozygotic) twins; opposite-sex twins; same-sex twins
bond or dependence and, 4, 232–233
conjoined twins, 227–228
genesis of, 223–225
polar body twins, 227
rates of twinning, 232
techniques for finding out, 4–5
terminology, 3–4
in utero development, 228–230